ANIMAL ETHICS

An in-depth exploration of an under-researched area with debates
much of the book [...] of animal' harm, from the pe
[...] rearing of animals, [...]
[...] the use of animals [...]
[...] animals [...]
[...] animal [...] and [...] a 'right to turn.' Tab
[...] are covered.

[...] animal [...] they are
[...] in [...] in agriculture?
[...] [...] species [...]
[...] in [...] in profit, testing, [...]
[...] animal [...] with other [...]

[...] some of the [...] as suggestions for fur
[...] this [...] an [...] an ideal book for [...]
[...] those [...] within [...] and interested
[...] others [...] be of [...]

[...] University of
Hertfordshire, UK.

The Basics

ANIMAL ETHICS
THE BASICS

Tony Milligan

Routledge
Taylor & Francis Group

LONDON AND NEW YORK

First published 2015
by Routledge
2 Park Square, Milton Park, Abingdon, Oxon OX14 4RN

and by Routledge
711 Third Avenue, New York, NY 10017

Routledge is an imprint of the Taylor & Francis Group, an informa business

© 2015 Tony Milligan

The right of Tony Milligan to be identified as author of this work has been asserted by him in accordance with sections 77 and 78 of the Copyright, Designs and Patents Act 1988.

British Library Cataloguing in Publication Data
A catalogue record for this book is available from the British Library

Library of Congress Cataloging in Publication Data
Milligan, Tony.
Animal ethics : the basics / Tony Milligan.
pages cm. -- (The basics)
Includes index.
1. Animal rights. 2. Animal welfare--Moral and ethical aspects. I. Title.
HV4708.M548 2015
179'.3--dc23
2014046590

ISBN: 978-0-415-73935-1 (hbk)
ISBN: 978-0-415-73936-8 (pbk)
ISBN: 978-1-315-72856-8 (ebk)

Typeset in Bembo
by Taylor & Francis Books

Printed by Ashford Colour Press Ltd.

To Suzanne, who brings out the animal in me.

CONTENTS

INTRODUCTION

This is a book with a very specific focus. It is concerned primarily with the tradition of animal ethics which has emerged out of the writings of Peter Singer and Tom Regan, a tradition which is sympathetic to the plight of animals and critical of our attitudes towards them. For Singer, this means that some form of **animal liberation** is required, a counterpart to the liberation of the poor and the oppressed throughout the world. Regan, on the other hand, has come to embrace an imagery of **abolition** which draws parallels between the predicament of animals and that of slaves in the nineteenth-century US. But, in various respects, the utilitarian defence of animals (presented by Singer) and the rights theory (presented by Regan) have been deemed problematic. They are seen as going too far or not going far enough in the defence of animals. And this is as it should be. The approaches in question were first set out almost exactly forty years ago (slightly earlier in Singer's case, slightly later in the case of Regan). This is rather a long time for any ethical theory to stand in the spotlight without receiving a good deal of critical attention. Much of what follows will track the main lines of opposition and the ongoing search for a successor approach.

More specifically, during the past two decades attempts have been made to establish a new orthodoxy based around an approach known as **abolitionism** which has emerged and gained a substantial presence in the United States, but which has struggled to achieve a similar impact in Europe or in Australasia. At its heart is a suspicion about piecemeal reforms as a distraction and as a way in which a continuing system of animal harms is given an ethical veneer. This approach has cast itself as the true revolutionary, by comparison with Singer's more reformist position and by comparison with Regan's vacillation between reform and the genuine revolutionary item. (Regan's abolition will not strike all abolitionists as being sufficiently radical.) Yet I have tried to ensure that this particular argument, while present throughout, does not dominate the text. A great deal of ink has been spilt, and not all of it in the most understanding of tones or to any useful purpose, on these matters. And so, instead, I have tried to situate abolitionism as one influential response to the perceived weaknesses of the Singer/Regan paradigm amongst others.

The final chapter, in particular, tries to explore the attempts to move towards a new position, in a sense a new orthodoxy, which is altogether more pragmatic than traditional animal liberation or abolitionism and yet is still insistent on the need for far-reaching changes in excess of welfare measures. The approaches in question form an important part of what is known as the **political turn** in animal ethics, in part because of the attention which they give to key concepts of liberal democratic politics, such as justice, liberty, equality, citizenship and democracy itself. In part, the label also arises because the approaches in question provide the theoretical backdrop for a more pragmatic animal rights movement, geared towards engagement with the political process rather than simply vegetarian or vegan outreach. The shared usual goal is the securing of actual and significant legislative change.

With this in mind, although the primary focus of the book is on ethical theories, it also tries to give readers some indication of how attitudes within the animal rights movement (alternatively, the animal liberation movement) have evolved since Singer first published his seminal *Animal Liberation* in 1975. To make sense of the theories, and what drives them, it is important to know that most activists, or **animal advocates** as they are generally known, have favoured Regan and a rights approach, rather than Singer's utilitarian, interest-based ethic. And it is helpful to know that abolitionism, in turn, emerged in response to a sense of disappointment about our limited progress towards the goals which Singer and Regan envisaged. It is also useful to know that theoretical tensions between animal rights and ecology have not been matched by the kind of deep divisions amongst activists that we might expect if the theoretical tensions were as deep as has sometimes been claimed.

These are the inclusions. What has been left out is an assortment of applied matters, argumentation which is more detailed than an introduction requires, alternative formulations of key points, and discussions which are still in an embryonic state. A range of familiar applied ethical topics such as 'What is wrong with factory farming?' and 'Is animal experimentation ethical?' have not been touched on, although the now dominant justification for ethically informed meat-eating has been dealt with. Rather, what follows presupposes that Singer and Regan were correct to hold that a case can be made against some, all or many instances of animal use. The reasonable debate then is about how extensive the critique of such practices should be. And so, while this is an introduction to animal ethics, it does not attempt to walk the reader through the need for the most rudimentary forms of ethical concern. It is presupposed that the reader will, for example, hold cruelty to be wrong and harm to be, in general, undesirable.

While the legacy of Singer and Regan has mostly been worked out within the tradition of **analytic philosophy** (with its concern for clearly set out argument structures) it would be odd to ignore the fascinating and important work which has emerged from the rival tradition of **continental philosophy**. While the former has tended to focus on one or two big concepts as a guide to animal ethics, the latter has pressed the case for deploying a broader set of concepts, and not just rights, or interests, or even justice. Engagement with the latter, and especially writings by Jacques Derrida and Donna Haraway, is more intermittent, but a necessary counterpart if we are to understand the key influences on current discussions of the Singer/Regan legacy. This rival tradition has a rigor of a different sort and offers insights which it would be difficult to ignore and which have already, to some extent, been taken up by analytic philosophers. Most importantly, while Singer and Regan focus on the inherent properties of individuals as a basis for making sense of their ethical standing, continental texts have tended to focus more on relations between humans and animals. As the analytic/continental divide has become blurred over the course of time, a more relational approach has also come to form a key line of analytic criticism of the first-generation theories.

The opening chapter provides an overview of the two broad approaches which have, as a result, now come to dominate animal ethics. On the one hand, there are approaches which unify various considerations by appeal to a key idea or cluster of ideas (such as rights or interests). Such approaches are explicit about their practical implications. On the other hand, there are more relational approaches which have a somewhat open texture and which give less explicit practical guidance. Chapters 2 and 3, respectively, set out the positions of Singer and Regan (instances of the former approach) together with some of the key criticisms which they have faced. Chapter 4 explores attempts to make sense of matters more relationally, by integrating animal ethics into mainstream ethico-political theory through the idea of a **social contract**. This contract idea is explored, firstly, as a rival way to underpin animal rights, and then as a possible justification for ethically informed meat-eating. Chapter 5 looks at the question of 'What, if anything, is so important about humans?' We seem to find the very idea of **species egalitarianism**—the idea that all animals are equal—to be implausible. But it is not obvious that we have any clear way to justify our human-prioritizing attitudes. Yet at the same time, a sense that humans matter in a special way is very difficult to get away from. It is perhaps ineradicable.

Chapter 6 extends this theme of the specialness of humans and harm to humans by looking at the most controversial (even offensive) analogy which animal rights supporters have deployed: the **Holocaust analogy**, with its suggestion that the industrial slaughter of animals has parallels with the most extreme and most obviously intolerable harm to which humans have subjected other humans. If the killing of a human and the killing of an animal are much the same then we may have an eternal Treblinka going on in our midst. Yet the analogy itself may easily be misunderstood, or dismissed on the basis of a misunderstanding. It is not obvious that it is deployed in an attempt to draw attention to an equivalence of harms, but rather to draw attention to a similarity in patterns of evasion (a widespread knowledge of wrongdoing is apparently coupled with an unwillingness to face the enormity of the wrong done).

Chapter 7 directly addresses the abolitionist position and its inter-connected commitments to a strong form of species egalitarianism, the extinction of domesticated creatures (including pets) and an end to the property status of animals. It also explores the driving considerations which give this position its appeal, the reasons why its impact has been geographically limited, and the fracture lines which are now resulting in the emergence of multiple forms of abolitionism rather than a single cohesive platform. Chapter 8 explores the continuities and discontinuities between advocacy of animal rights and ecological concern. The key area of tension is over **individualism** versus **holism**. While there is a strong ecological case for vegetarian and vegan diets, animal advocacy has tended to follow Singer and Regan by focusing on individual creatures as the basic unit of value. Ecologists, by contrast, take ecosystems as their ethically basic units. Yet this tension can be, and perhaps has been, overstated, and the broader division between individualism and communitarianism which sits in the background may be similarly insecure.

Chapter 9 continues with this theme of the limits of the contrast between individual and community in the context of an exploration of the political turn. It examines attempts to situate animals in relation to the political community, standards of justice, and liberal norms such as liberty, equality and the avoidance of cruelty. The chapter draws attention to the fact that fraternity has been steadily downgraded within liberal political thought and to the suggestion (by Jacques Derrida and others) that this ultimately yields an impoverished con-ception of the political which is, of necessity, always enacted within the context of some or other community. Yet political communities provide a context where interests are not simply considered, but considered as part of the **common good**. The various difficulties of situating animals in relation to this common good, and doing so in an ethically defensible but effectively pragmatic manner, are challenging.

Key terms are highlighted in bold when first used in the text and (for the sake of the reader who wishes to dip into particular chapters) when first used in any particular chapter. A glossary of these terms is supplied at the end of the text. The terms in question are often focal points for discussions and disagreements in the literature on animal ethics, and their precise definition is a matter of controversy. The primary purpose of the definitions given in the Glossary is, therefore, to allow the reader to understand the text, they are not intended as an attempt to settle these disagreements, especially where the latter concern the fine-tuning of our concepts.

As with all books, this one owes more debts than can be or ought to be acknowledged. I should, however, like to recognize my special indebtedness to colleagues who have participated in successive MANCEPT (Manchester Centre for Political Theory) workshops on 'Animals and Political Theory' at the University of Manchester and successive panels on animals and ethics at the Society for Applied Philosophy Conference, firstly at the University of Zurich in 2013, and then at St Anne's College, Oxford, in the summer of 2014. In particular, Alasdair Cochrane, Steve Cooke, Rob Garner, John Hadley and Siobhan O'Sullivan have helped to improve the quality of my understanding of the political turn, while bearing no responsibility for the productive or unproductive flaws within my own position. Their writings have also been an ongoing source of illumination and direction. A further debt is owed to my students at the universities of Aberdeen, Hull and Hertfordshire, for teaching me more about animal ethics than I could have hoped to learn on my own; to Siobhán Poole and Iram Satti at Routledge for accepting that a book genuinely was emerging, in spite of the lack of tangible evidence; and to my wife, Suzanne, who has shown more patience than I deserved during the final days of writing (and at other times also).

1

PICTURING ANIMAL ETHICS

There are two main approaches towards animal ethics. On the one hand, there are theories which focus on a small cluster of key considerations or even on a single big idea such as rights, suffering or sentience. They are unifying approaches. On the other hand, there are theories which insist on situating animals within a broader ethical context, usually the context of a set of historically constructed practices which bind humans and animals together and which at the same time generate a sense of separateness. These are relational approaches. The former are appealing because they are streamlined, efficient and aim at precision. They tend to offer determinate answers to otherwise difficult questions such as 'When, if ever, should we allow ourselves to eat meat?' If the central concept which we work with is that of rights or harm then the answer to this question is straightforward: all other things being equal, we ought not to eat meat whenever doing so would involve a rights violation or whenever it would promote significant harm. If, by contrast, we base our ethic around some unifying standard that animals do not satisfy (such as a requirement for our kind of language use) then our ethic will tell us that we are entitled to continue meat-eating, to continue experimentation, and to continue various forms of animal incarceration. We may then be licensed to act in much the same ways that we have done in the past, especially if we abide by some reasonable welfare constraints to avoid unnecessary harm (to animals) or psychological distress (to ourselves and others).

In either case, by appeal to some basic consideration or small cluster of considerations, unifying approaches allow dilemmas to be reduced or eliminated and they tell us which practices are licensed and which are excluded. If we like our ethics to be determinate rather than uncertain or imprecise this is a definite advantage. Ethicists who work in the tradition of **analytic philosophy**, where lucidity and argument structures are given top priority, have tended to favour this option.

By contrast, more relational approaches tend also to be more discursive and somewhat harder to inhabit. They require deliberation of a different sort, often without any guarantee that a single final answer can be given to any particular question. Differing relational approaches may also 'talk past' one another, without acknowledging clear ways in which disputes may be settled. In these respects, they lack the charm of simplicity but instead, as compensation, they may claim to do greater justice to how the world is and to what human life is like. Relational approaches also tend to be more influenced by **continental philosophy**, and by the idea that picturing, rather than streamlined argument, is philosophy's most important task. While this may involve precision, it is a different kind of precision from the sort that we find in the big unifying theories. And it is a kind of precision which may only be evident from the inside of this sort of discourse. From the outside, it may appear to be irreducibly messy.

This contrast of these two approaches is (like the contrast between analytic and continental philosophy) a simplification. The lines between the two approaches often blur under the pressure of dialogue and disagreement. But the sympathies of those who try to think seriously about animals, from an ethical point of view, do tend to lean towards one or other option. And where our own personal sympathies lie may tell us a good deal about ourselves. Even so, much of what follows will presuppose that both approaches are insightful enough to deserve our attention. There is, surely, a place for large, unifying ideas which can be rolled out across the entire field of enquiry—in the process generating close and persuasive argumentation. But there is also a place for context, for the messiness of the particular and for deliberations which may sway opinion without ever amounting to a conclusive proof. It is arguable that ethics in general, and not just animal ethics, is always like this. That is to say, it is always a cluster of different sorts of things: ways of arguing, ways of picturing, ways of shaping action and advice—sometimes clear and sometimes elusive. It would certainly be odd for someone with a deep interest in contemporary animal ethics to draw only and exclusively from one side of the divide. Yet the divide is real, if blurred, and attempts to talk across it do not always succeed.

UNIFYING APPROACHES

What I have called unifying approaches are not, of course, restricted to the use of a single concept. Rather, they make everything revolve around one central (unifying) idea or theme which is then repeatedly deployed. The best-known and most influential work of this sort comes from Peter Singer (who focuses on suffering as a basis for **moral considerability**); Tom Regan (who appeals to the pivotal importance of animals being **subjects-of-a-life**); and Gary Francione (who appeals to sentience as all that is required for moral standing). All three emphasize particular kinds of continuity between humans and other animals. They also consider the fact that *we* are human and *they* are not, to have no special ethical importance. For Singer, Regan and Francione, it is no more important than the fact that I have brown eyes while someone else may have blue eyes. The ethically salient considerations, the things that really matter for the purposes of deliberation and decision, are taken to be considerations of a quite different sort. They are taken to be considerations of the following sort: like us, a large range of animals suffer; many lead lives which are psychologically integrated and are not simply a mass of fleeting events; like us, such animals are beings who have the capacity for experience of a robust sort, although it is not necessarily the exact same kind of experience.

Of the three pivotal thinkers mentioned above, Regan and Francione are influenced by the deontological (rights- and duty-focused) tradition of Immanuel Kant (1724–1804) while Singer is influenced by the utilitarian tradition of Jeremy Bentham (1748–1832) and John Stuart Mill (1806–1873). Regan and Francione claim that animals have rights which we regularly violate and which, instead, we should respect, while Singer focuses instead on consequences rather than rights. For Singer, we should set aside unhelpful and contentious rights talk and instead try to secure the best overall outcome for our actions. Deliberation about what makes something a good outcome should, however, take animal interests into account, and for Singer, it should take such interests to be equal in importance to our own, human interests. (Although, what this means in practice turns out to be a little less radical than we might expect.) In addition to detailed criticisms of the sort which will be set out in subsequent chapters, and in spite of their differences, all three thinkers face a number of shared and general objections to their approaches. The objections are general in the sense that while they can occur in the context of deliberation about animals, they are not specifically or exclusively about animal ethics but, rather, they concern how we should go about the business of any kind of ethical deliberation. They are, ultimately, objections to the parent theories, respectively **Kantianism** and **utilitarianism**. The suggestion from critics is that such approaches are reductive or misleading about what it is to be an ethical agent, i.e. about what it is to act reasonably, on a day-to-day basis, in the light of ethical considerations.

Three objections of this sort stand out. The first involves an appeal to the complexity of experience; the second highlights a problematic separation of justification and motivation; and the third concerns a marginalizing of our humanity, a failure to accommodate the idea that being human is itself ethically salient.

The appeal to the complexity of experience charges that real, lived, experienced ethical deliberation is complex in ways that approaches such as Kantianism and utilitarianism do not comprehend. None of us live out our lives in a way which is shaped by commitment to a single overriding and guiding ethical consideration or norm, *no matter what that consideration or norm may happen to be*. Theories which suggest otherwise, which focus excessively on only one aspect of ethical life, promote what has (unflatteringly) been called 'moral Esperanto', a language of ethics that nobody speaks. As a point about what humans are like (i.e. most humans, people like us), we are invariably pluralists about ethical norms. In practice, when we have to make an important ethical choice, we factor in lots of different considerations and we do not always do so in the same way from case to case. This point applies even in cases of deliberation about suffering. The latter is a consideration which we might imagine will always play a single unwavering role, just in the way that harm does. The fact that something involves suffering, and hardship more generally, may be a reason to prevent it from occurring, and this is what we ordinarily assume to be true: suffering is to be avoided. However, the fact that something involves suffering may also function as a reason for bringing it about (as it does in the case of going to the North Pole or, less dramatically, walking the Inca Trail—both of which would require us to endure considerable hardship). Sometimes, we do things because they circumvent suffering, yet endurance in the face of suffering is a precondition for some kinds of accomplishment. And while it might be objected that the suffering in such cases is outweighed by the pleasure of accomplishment, the point remains that it is the adversity or the suffering itself which counts in favour of the action rather than against it. Focusing on suffering in the abstract then seems to miss the importance of the context in which it occurs.

Examples like this can be used to argue that an approach towards ethics (animal ethics or ethics of any sort) which centres too much on suffering, and on its avoidance, oversimplifies what our kind of life is like. It seems, to many ethicists, unable to account satisfactorily for large areas of what it is to be someone like us. A similar point can be made in the case of a single-minded focus on rights. Such an approach may seem to obscure and to lose sight of something important. And this point need not be a clever way of sidestepping the question of whether or not animals actually do have rights. It applies just as much when we think about humans. For example, let us imagine that a parent sells their child into prostitution because the going rate for children happens to be particularly favourable and not because they are in desperate straits and believe that prostitution is a better option for their child than starvation. There would be something distinctly odd about addressing this action *firstly* or *simply* in terms of rights and, relatedly, in terms of child protection. To capture a sense of what has gone wrong we might instead have to appeal, from the outset, to the idea of betrayal, to a very deep failure of parental responsibility, to the parent's heartlessness and perhaps also to a failure to love. If we do not do this, we may miss salient aspects of the situation, aspects which we need to see if we are to grasp more fully what is going on.

The point here is not that child protection and rights are dispensable or peripheral, any more than a concern for favourable consequences.

Rather, the point is that talk about rights and child protection needs to be situated within a broader picture of moral failure. And in order to perform this task we may need to see that this is not just the violation of a single important norm. Rather, we may need to see that something has gone wrong in the parent's entire way of relating to the child. If the offending parent was to say, in their defence, 'Of course, if I had known that my child had rights I would never have sold them', this would be a far from satisfactory response. It would, after all, be odd to imagine that relations between the parent and child were utterly normal, healthy and appropriate up to the point when the parent suddenly, and purely for gain, decided to realize their investment by transferring ownership.

And if rights talk, although indispensable, does not always go ethically deep enough in the case of humans then why should we expect it to do so in the case of animals? Indeed, an overemphasis on rights might seem to entrench a sense that the standing of animals is second-rate. While relations with fellow humans are accepted as complex, as governed by far more than rights, relations with non-humans would then seem to be adequately captured by a much simpler set of rule-like considerations. And this is exactly the kind of downgrading of animal status that animal advocates have been keen to avoid. (Both here, and throughout, I will refer to agents who argue for a radical alteration in our treatment of animals as **animal advocates**.)

The upshot is that a number of such advocates have pressed the need to go beyond animal rights if we are to set matters straight. A number of feminists, in particular, have sought to talk instead about an ethics of 'care' which is far less rule-like, and hence is less shaped by what is taken to be a male and rule-oriented perspective. Some of those who advance this position, such as Kathy Rudy in *Loving Animals: Towards a New Animal Advocacy* (2011), have appealed to the idea that rights talk is restrictive as a reason to entirely reject the idea of animal rights because it is too bound up with the prevailing (flawed) power relations: it does not reflect life experience, but rather, it reflects the experience of those who exert a gendered dominance. Others have pressed the same point only to restrict the application of talk about animal rights, allowing such talk to perform some important roles but not others.

The second objection to the parent theories which sit behind unifying approaches, the appeal to a separation of justification and motivation, involves a claim that they pose a threat to our integrity. Unifying approaches risk the danger of introducing a kind of ethical schizophrenia into our lives, a division between the justifications which we offer for our actions and the considerations which actually motivate us to act. Take a simple example. Suppose that we see someone beating a dog in the local public park and that we then decide to intervene on the animal's behalf. We might, if called on to explain our actions, appeal to the rights of the animal or to a concern with minimizing the overall amount of suffering in the world. We would not, of course, put matters in quite this way (it would sound too pompous), but we might nonetheless appeal to these considerations in a more roundabout manner.

However, it is not obvious that this would be at all plausible as an account of what has actually motivated our intervention. While it does seem possible that we might be motivated by the animal's suffering, it is very unlikely that we would be motivated directly, or primarily, by a concern for the amount of suffering in the world at large. Similarly, while the beating might well violate the animal's rights, it seems odd to suggest that we would be motivated by a concern for the upholding of rights rather than a concern for the animal itself. The sheer callous cruelty of the action, or compassion for this particular suffering creature, and more especially unease with the occurrence of harm before our very eyes, would be far more likely candidates for factors which might have helped to shape our response.

This might, nonetheless, seem like a rather academic or legalistic point. Even if justification and motivation do fall apart this fact may seem unimportant just so long as we end up *doing the right thing*. However, matters are not quite so simple. There are many things which each of us ought to do but which we do not do, for one reason or another. Partly, this is a matter of our just being human and, as such, it is something which we must accept if we are to live at all well. But partly, it is a matter of our engaging in ethical deliberation in ways which fail to motivate. This can be a way of evading matters which, arguably, we *ought* to be motivated by, which are entirely consistent with living well and enjoying a good life. It is an odd reflection, but nonetheless a realistic one, that we are not always moved to act on things that we consider to be wrong. This motivation problem is regularly commented on in the context of both animal ethics and environmental ethics and it was identified by Peter

Singer, some years ago, in the opening introduction to his classic *Animal Liberation* (1975). Singer tried to address the puzzle of why there are people (many people) who accept the arguments for vegetarianism but who do not go on to change their diet or their lives. Instead, the arguments seem to have no practical impact. This may lead us to question the value of ethics or at least the value of ethical theory. Surely, it has to do more than allow us to pass exams or to identify ourselves with one philosophical tradition rather than another. Even worse, the formal acceptance of an argument (about the standing of animals, or about anything whatsoever) can function as a way of setting the matter aside, as something resolved and requiring no more deliberation.

Part of the reason for this failure of at least some arguments to motivate may be that we are fickle, which, of course, we are. But it seems unlikely that this can account for the problem as a whole. Alternatively, it may then be tempting to adopt general theory about the very nature of motivation and judgement, one which severs reasoning and motivation, beliefs and desires, so that each becomes quite separate from the other (a view which makes it difficult to understand why at least some beliefs do seem to motivate, even when we wish matters were otherwise). Or finally, it might be argued that deliberation which regularly fails to motivate, which merely runs parallel to motivation, is simply deliberation of the wrong sort. If the goal of animal advocates is to actually change our behaviour, then there may well be a good case for embracing the latter option.

In addition to the above concerns, there is a widespread suspicion that unifying approaches, by focusing so much on suffering, consequences or rights, tend not only to obscure the complexities of what is involved in being an ethical agent, but also to obscure important and ethically defensible differences between our attitudes towards other animals and our attitudes towards other humans. They involve what we might call a marginalizing of our humanity. If, for example, all that ultimately matters is suffering, or qualifying as a bearer of rights, or being sentient, then the mere fact that someone happens to be a fellow human automatically seems to be irrelevant. To talk about any special relation or special obligation that we have to other humans may even seem to be an instance of species bias or what has become known as **speciesism**. The way in which the best-known unifying theories are set up, from the outset, seems to quite deliberately bar any sense that our shared humanity is ethically salient. Yet the idea that our humanity does matter is a consideration which is extremely difficult to get away from. It may seem easy to send it into exile but this is an exile who keeps returning, albeit in unacknowledged and unexpected ways. It is hard, perhaps psychologically impossible, for a normal, human, ethical agent to truly escape from a sense of the ethical importance of *being human*. Psychopaths may do so rather more easily, but they provide a poor model for ethical agency.

As well as a concern about the psychological unavailability of such an escape from the importance of humanity, there are considerations of realpolitik which come into play. Humans are seen as having an almost unquestionable special standing in the minds of most moral agents and this is something which is unlikely to end anytime soon. Perhaps an effective real-world ethic cannot run too far ahead of the civilization in which it is embedded. Theories which ignore this may risk marginalization. They may fail to connect up with what most of us feel to be important and action-guiding. Our ethical task then may not be one of deliberating as if we were utterly neutral about species membership, but rather it may be the task of figuring out what is due to *other* creatures and what it is *to be human* in the species sense or in some other sense which involves being part of a human moral community—a community which is, and has been, the beneficiary of great and many harms to non-humans. And this is a way of looking at matters which takes us closer to the heart of relational approaches where the appeal of streamlined argument construction is sacrificed in favour of the complexities of picturing human/animal continuity, difference and interconnection.

RELATIONAL APPROACHES

Whereas approaches which centre around one big idea tend to emphasize the similarities between humans and non-humans, more relational and discursive approaches tend to emphasize the *otherness* of animals. The latter are not just diminished or restricted approximations to the human, they are in constant relation with us yet (in many respects) they are also very different. Examples of such other-emphasizing approaches include the work of Cora Diamond, Jacques Derrida and Donna Haraway. In a number of influential essays, the most-quoted of which is 'Eating Meat and Eating People', Diamond tries to explore the ways in which the concepts which we use to make sense of our connection to animals have conceptions of value built in. When, for example, we refer to some animals as 'vermin' we are not using a special, value-neutral biological classification. When we then go on to deliberate about what can and cannot be done to vermin, the discussion is already loaded against them because, to see any animal as vermin is already, from the outset, to see the animal as placed beyond the ordinary rules—even, to an extent, the rules which govern cruelty. Things can be done to them which cannot be done in other cases. This understanding of the very idea, the very concept of 'vermin', makes a good deal of sense when we think about attempts to represent humans as vermin, as beyond the ordinary rules and standards, and hence as fair game for eradication. Similarly, we may think of the hunting of foxes on the grounds that they are vermin. The animals are deliberately torn apart by a pack of dogs which are specially bred and reared for this very purpose. Only in relation to creatures who stand outside of the regular rules would this be accepted. Yet this way of classifying, which comes to have the apparent force of a neutral biological category, is in fact a claim of entitlement, an entitlement to harm in otherwise impermissible ways is already built into the concept.

A similar case is provided by the classification of some animals as 'lab animals' in spite of the fact that they are biologically the same as animals which are not experimented on but are, instead, household pets. The classification alone involves a conception of what these creatures exist *for*—they are there specifically to be sources of information. And given this, what we can do to a creature which is a lab animal is again taken to be quite different from what we can do to a creature which is a pet, although they may both be dogs, or cats or rabbits or mice. The 'lab animal' classification sanctions a glaring inconsistency in our modes of responding. The more favoured side of this inconsistency concerns those animals which we regard as 'pets'. Pethood comes with special sorts of protection and privileges which are not afforded to other animals. The very idea of a pet, or at least the enriched version of the concept which we ordinarily work with, is not that of a creature who just happens to be bought and sold in a pet store, and it is not simply that of a creature for whom someone holds a licence or claim of ownership. Rather, to regard an animal as a pet is already to see it as a creature with whom a human might share aspects of their life, it is to see it as a creature with whom we might bond, perhaps even in deep ways. Diamond also believes that a prohibition of consumption is built into the concept. To see a creature as a pet is already to see it as a being who cannot be eaten, although the possibility of honorific consumption (which occurs in other cultures) seems to be missing from this picture. A qualification to this reading of the concept of the pet is that pethood is still somewhat tainted through its association with property, with the idea that this is *my* pet, and not yours. Animal advocates tend, therefore, to refer instead to 'companion animals' who have 'animal guardians' rather than owners. In some parts of the US, legal standing for this classification has been secured. This draws on the more positive side of the concept of pethood while removing some of its unwelcome historical connotations.

To see a creature as livestock is again very different: it is to see it as a creature which exists *in order to be* eaten—that is its *raison d'être*, just as the *raison d'être* of a lab animal is to be subjected to experimentation and to yield information as a result. And so, we can see a repeated pattern in which our very ways of conceptualizing, of picturing other creatures, come with inbuilt norms, inbuilt permissions and requirements. Diamond's big move is to point out that this applies not only to non-human animals but to humans also. There is a familiar biological idea of the human, an idea of species membership, of being one of the *Homo sapiens*, of being a creature with a genetic code which varies only very slightly from case to case. But the term is also used in a quite different way, to indicate what we and others are due. To see someone as a human, in this sense, is to rule out various kinds of action. It is to see them as someone who is worthy of care and consideration precisely because they are a fellow human. A classic example of this is given by George Orwell in *A Homage to Catalonia* (1938). Orwell describes his time as a volunteer, fighting against fascism with the international brigades during the Spanish Civil War. Watching the enemy caught by surprise, he describes a man scurrying for his life with his trousers still at his ankles, a man he does not try to shoot. The reason given is that he does not see the enemy or a fascist, but simply a fellow human caught up in a much greater conflict. This way of regarding others—as beings with whom we share a common humanity—is neither the mere recognition of species membership nor is it a natural given. It is a product of centuries and more of human history.

It is, for those such as Diamond and Raimond Gaita, a historical accomplishment which we should be cautious about trying to unravel. But it is also an accomplishment which is open to use against the non-human. As we shall see in subsequent chapters, Peter Singer and Tom Regan have repeatedly warned about the dangers of speciesism as an indefensible pro-human bias which is comparable to racism, anti-Semitism and sexism and we may suspect that all this talk about the human simply *is* just such a prejudice. For Diamond, on the other hand, it is precisely *this* sense of a shared humanity which has helped, in the past, to undermine both racism and anti-Semitism—although they remain residually powerful forces and have the capacity to flourish under favourable circumstances. If this sense of a shared humanity, a shared human bond, has played such a positive role then it is not something that we should thoughtlessly seek to undermine even in the name of impartiality or **species egalitarianism**—a concept which can be understood and articulated in different ways. It is unlikely that a rise in racism or any other kind of prejudice, by humans against other humans, would in any way help to move society towards a better treatment of animals. The possibility of some form of animal liberation, or at least the recognition of an extensive system of animal rights, seems to require that various liberal norms, such as a broadly egalitarian way of humans seeing one another, are already in place. And so the concern then is that any attack on the idea that our humanity matters may compromise something of strategic importance to the animal cause. What we then seem to need, at least from Diamond's point of view, is not arguments for species neutrality but, rather, firstly, a recognition that we relate to non-humans not just as individuals but as members of a human community, and secondly we need a conception of how to *be* human in a way which can restrict and perhaps help us to eradicate familiar forms of animal harm.

Here, we can see how a more relational attitude shapes a sense of what matters ethically in a way which runs counter to the unifying approaches of Singer and Regan. But Diamond is still closely related to their tradition of philosophy. Specifically, she draws on the work of Ludwig Wittgenstein whose own writings were first an articulation of, and then a rebellion against, the analytic tradition of philosophy.

If we look further away from this analytic tradition we can find a deep questioning, a deconstruction or constructive pulling apart of the idea of the human as privileged. Jacques Derrida's *The Animal That Therefore I Am* (2006) is an exemplary continental examination of our sense that humans stand above animals. Like Diamond, Derrida acknowledges the importance of our sense of humanity, a sense of the importance of being human which does not seem to go away. But he draws out respects in which this sense of humanity has not emerged in splendid isolation. Rather, it involves an understanding of ourselves *by contrast with* creatures who are not human. In a sense, it is these creatures who are other than us who make possible our humanity, our sense of who and what we are. In a characteristically intriguing and complex formulation, Derrida sums up his attitude towards the human/animal boundary. 'Everything I'll say will consist, certainly not in effacing the limit, but in multiplying its figures, in complicating, thickening, delinearizing, folding, and dividing the line precisely by making it increase and multiple.' This is an elusive way of putting matters, but we may still get the point: the sense that there is a boundary does not get removed, but what sits on either side of the boundary is grasped through what sits on the other side. Indeed, for Derrida, even the fact that we refer to all living creatures which are not human as 'animals' is absurdly reductive. It lumps together whales and spiders, scallops and antelope by appeal simply to their non-humanity. This seems almost lazy, a way of ensuring that we miss the particularity of individual creatures from the outset.

At the heart of Derrida's approach is a reversal of the order of things. He asks not how we see the animal, but how we are seen by the animal, and not by some abstract animal but by a particular animal. Echoing the beginnings of Western discourse on our supremacy through a play on the shame of nakedness in Eden, he describes himself stepping wet out of the shower and, caught in the act by his cat, Derrida experiences embarrassment. But this is an instructive moment, a recognition that this is a creature *in its own right*, one before whom he can feel embarrassment, shame and many other things besides. Yet it is *his* cat, not just any cat but a particular cat with whom he is in relation—indeed it is his cat but, in truth, they are *together* in a meaningful relationship. There are multiple themes in play here, and one is the non-biographical point: it is always a particular creature who can gaze on us, just as we as individuals can gaze on them. This particularity of the moment of encounter matters. Just as there is an immense difference between a horse and a mouse (yet both of them are 'animals') so there is an immense difference between one cat and another, or one horse and another, or (we might add) one human and another. The reduction of other beings, in their complex creatureliness, to undifferentiated units of the same skews our ethical deliberations and it does so unfavourably: uniqueness is arbitrarily reserved for humans while animals are seen as interchangeable units. (This is a view which, as we shall see, surfaces in both ethically informed defences of meat-eating and in Peter Singer's utilitarian defence of animal interests.)

This might seem, and has seemed to some, a projection of individuality, liberalism and all the machinery of Western capitalist ideology onto the non-human. Gilles Deleuze and Félix Guattari, writing in *A Thousand Plateaus: Capitalism and Schizophrenia* (1980) long before Derrida, but in a relatedly continental philosophical tradition, once attacked any such focus as bourgeois individualism, an attack which targets the household owner/pet relation as an epitome of bourgeois control. (Wild animals fare better—a feature, as we shall see, also of some ecological discourses.) Derrida's repetitive insistence that he encounters *his* cat, and not just any cat, may then seem to have fallen into this trap. It may seem to be little more than the sentimental peddling of bourgeois ideology, or at least a surrender to the consolations of hearth and home where one can live out a fantasy relation to some particular instance of a type of creature. Yi-Fu Tuan's *Dominance and Affection: The Making of Pets* (1984) pursues a more liberally minded version of the same point: affection for pets is the flip side of dominance and not an alternative to it. Affection for pets is always implicated in the dominant forms of power and control. For Tuan, this means that, although humans have kept animals for a very long time, the modern pet is not actually the same as the historic pet of antiquity (any more than the power relations of modernity and those of antiquity are the same). Rather, the modern pet is a compensation for the atomization and difficulty of emotional expression which emerged with industrialization in the nineteenth century. Affection from and towards pets comes without the usual vulnerabilities associated with human–human relations because the pet itself is thoroughly constructed by the alienated human. Rather than finding something ethically instructive in our relation as individuals to individual domestic creatures (creatures such as Derrida's cat) the latter yield only a microcosm of such human alienation and the felt need for both affection and control.

Among commentators who try to look more sympathetically at Derrida's focus on the irreducible individuality of the creatures with whom we are in relation, one of the most prominent and effective challengers of the idea of the human is Donna Haraway. She takes up Derrida's point about the irreducible relatedness of the human to its other, to the non-human, but she is nonetheless critical of Derrida's apparent failure to address how the animal itself (any particular other creature such as Derrida's cat) actually sees the human, and the capabilities and capacities that it can bring to bear. For Haraway, the old Deleuzian unwillingness to come to terms with the particularity of creatures is misleading, yet Derrida's own, particularity-recognizing account seems to be altogether too focused on the human side of the relation, albeit it is a focus on the human seen in the light of the animal. But if we do not actually address the standpoint of the latter, how any animal actually sees rather than how we feel when seen, a deceptively extended divide will remain. By contrast, the more we know about the actual standpoint of non-human others, the more we will realize that Derrida is right after all and that we have our being in relation to them. For Haraway, this is an evolutionary point as well as a conceptual one. We are evolutionary partners. Yet this is rarely acknowledged. Instead, there is the narrative in which humanity makes itself and then proceeds to make the domesticated dog, remodelling a wild creature (the wolf) in order to do so. The narrative, we now know, is flawed in all sorts of ways. Significant differentiation, the beginnings of the dog by contrast with the wolf, occurred prior to domestication, far earlier than the tale can allow. The point of such creation narratives is to show *us* controlling and making *them* rather than the kind of reciprocal arrangement, the *evolving with*, which Haraway and Derrida each in their different ways try to draw out. The creation narratives are very Western, very Judaeo-Christian, and they shape our understanding of both the human and the non-human. And so, while Derrida and Haraway do not agree with Deleuze's Marxist-influenced hostility to the particular domestic animal, they nonetheless engage in social critique.

Discussions of this sort—attempts to situate the idea of the human and the non-human—suggest that, when we come to set up arguments for or against animal rights, or for or against any particular kind of animal harm, most of the important work has already been done. It has been done through our representations of the creatures (humans and non-humans) we are supposed to be comparing. Arguments which conflict with the relevant value-laden representations are liable to be ignored, set aside or (at best) accepted as fine in theory but inapplicable in practice. The suggestion then, from relational approaches, is that picturing *realistically*, or *justly*, or in ways which rein in our anthropocentric (speciesist) bias, may be ethically more basic than argument-building. But here we may wonder if this is rather too quick and convenient a claim, a way of setting aside the force of compelling arguments which may often convey simple but uncomfortable truths which relational accounts do not clearly affirm. More specifically, as with the unifying approaches, there are substantial objections which can be raised against the kind of open-ended, discursive approach to human/animal relations that we find in Diamond, Derrida and Haraway.

Firstly, such approaches may grasp a sense of our difference from animals, and the difference of animals from each other. But they are evasive about key points of ethical continuity, such as our shared capacities for consciousness and suffering, i.e. the features which unifying accounts tend to focus on. Because of this, they are prone to feed into and compromise with established prejudices which treat animals as standing outside and beyond the ordinary ethical considerations which humans recognize in our dealings with each other.

Secondly, discourses of this sort may be edifying and illuminating, but because of their multiple ambiguities and focus on 'problematizing' they are insufficiently action-guiding. They do not actually tell us whether or not we can eat animals, experiment on them or keep them as pets. Indeed, it is striking that while Cora Diamond has presented her approach as a way of critiquing our mistreatment of animals, as part of a case for vegetarianism and against animal experimentation, others who draw from the same themes have not seen matters in quite the same way. The Australian philosopher, Raimond Gaita, who draws on Diamond's conceptual insights, uses them to emphasize the importance of our sense of a common humanity. But for Gaita, our lives are meaningful while the lives of animals are lacking in meaning. To draw out some determinate personal or public-policy guidelines which might make their way into law, something closer to the precision of the unifying accounts may be required.

Finally, it may be suspected that strongly relational and deliberative approaches may also be guilty of misdirecting our attention. Instead of focusing on the actual suffering of animals, the dreadful harms to which they are subject, such accounts remain caught up in the idea that we humans are something special, that being human or being human in relation to non-humans is a deep and meaningful enigma. In a sense, this is Haraway's worry about Derrida but applied more generally to relational accounts as a whole: by focusing on the complex problems of being human, and on the relation of animal to human, the standpoint of the animal itself gets lost.

CONCLUSION

While there is a significant difference between what I have called unifying approaches and what I have referred to as relational approaches, each has been able to generate considerable disagreement in a process of critique and counter-critique. The relational accounts seem to have, as their main advantage, an ability to capture far more of the complex experience of being a human confronted by non-human creatures, but the unifying approaches have the advantage of being more obviously action-guiding. It is this which helps to explain why they continue to be more attractive to animal advocates and to organizations which seek to redress various instances of conspicuous animal harm. In a sense, animal ethics modelled on variants of the positions represented by Singer, Regan and even Francione may suffer from some general difficulties which are carried over from their parent theories (Kantianism and utilitarianism) but they are tailor-made for activist movements. By contrast, an ethic for human/animal relations which is shaped by approaches such as those of Diamond, Derrida and Haraway will have the advantage of meshing well with sophisticated social critiques, but far more difficulty connecting to a practice of animal advocacy or to the pursuit of some form of animal liberation.

FURTHER READING

Donna Haraway's *The Companion Species Manifesto* (Chicago: Prickly Paradigm Press, 2003) and *When Species Meet* (Minneapolis: University of Minnesota Press, 2008) set animal ethics in a relational context. Peter Singer's *Animal Liberation* (London: Random House, 1995 [1975]) together with Tom Regan's *The Case for Animal Rights* (Berkeley: University of California Press, 2004) and the critique of the latter in Gary Francione's *Animals as Persons: Essays on the Abolition of Animal Exploitation* (New York: Columbia University Press, 2008) try to unify animal ethics by appeal to a small cluster of core concepts.

Jacques Derrida's *The Animal That Therefore I Am* (New York: Fordham University Press, 2008 [2006]) is the seminal continental examination of human/animal relations. For a good, accessible outline of Derrida's position see Erica Fudge's *Pets* (Stockfield: Acumen, 2008). For a contrastingly hostile attitude towards animal companionship see Gilles Deleuze and Félix Guattari, *A Thousand Plateaus: Capitalism and Schizophrenia* (London: Continuum, 2003 [1980]).

Cora Diamond, *The Realistic Spirit* (Cambridge, MA: MIT Press, 1991), contains her relationally focused essays on meat-eating and experimentation. Raimond Gaita's *A Common Humanity* (London: Routledge, 2000) picks up on Diamond's Wittgensteinian approach but the tone is less sympathetic to non-humans. For a more analytically inclined formulation of a relational approach, see Claire Palmer's *Animal Ethics in Context* (New York: Columbia University Press, 2010).

Kathy Rudy's *Loving Animals: Towards a New Animal Advocacy* (Minneapolis: University of Minnesota Press, 2011) sets out a feminist-influenced critique of the rights approach, combined with a defence of ethically informed meat-eating. Vicky Hearne's article 'What's Wrong with Animal Rights?', *Harper's Magazine*, September 1991, pp. 59–64, gives a concise and influential statement of traditional animal rights theory's blindness to the relational dimensions of ethics. For a quite different feminist approach which is more sympathetic to a rights approach, see Carol Adams, *The Sexual Politics of Meat*, Twentieth Anniversary Edition (London: Continuum, 2010), which attempts to track connections between meat-eating, misogyny and conceptions of masculinity. The Adams book is both controversial and a celebrated text. Yi-Fu Tuan's anthropological study, *Dominance and Affection: The Making of Pets* (New Haven: Yale University Press, 1984), holds a similarly established status and has an impressive historical sweep.

2

SINGER'S UTILITARIANISM

Although there have been a number of important, pioneering, texts on the ethical standing of animals, and more particularly on animal rights, the point of origin for contemporary discussions of animal ethics is Peter Singer's **utilitarian** defence of animal interests in *Animal Liberation* (1975). Singer's text followed a sustained wave of activism and a series of public exposés of indefensible practices in the food and experimentation systems. The combined impact of this activism, and an increased public awareness of animal harms, was a temporary curtailment of experimentation together with greater oversight of (and publicity-sensitivity to) the food system. Buoyed by initial indications of progress, Singer's text was quickly adopted as the theoretical underpinning of the emerging animal rights move-ment. Yet, paradoxically, Singer was not, and is not, a rights theorist. At the heart of his position is a critique of the assumption—for Singer, a speciesist assumption—that human interests matter more than animal interests. Indeed, the analytical portion of the book (which, overall, consists largely of disturbing empirical detail about animal harms) is built around the claim that *all creatures are equal*. The sense in which they (we) are taken to be equal does, however, have to be clarified and is subject to heavy qualification. The point, for Singer, is that all creatures are equally entitled to have their interests taken into account, whenever they happen to have interests. Failure to abide by this principle of the equal consideration of interests was, and for Singer remains, a form of **speciesism**.

The concept of speciesism, of a certain kind of species-based prejudice, is itself rather complex and underexplained in the Singer text. The reader must fill in a good many gaps. Partly, it involves favouring the members of one species over the members of one or more other species and doing so for reasons which are not accidental but rather are based on their species membership. Talk about prejudice of this sort is rather broader than talk about **anthropocentrism** (favouring humans) although the two are related. In theory, the victims of speciesism could actually be humans, if there were some powerful species around to dominate us, or if someone was so misanthropic that they happened to favour non-humans instead. Similarly, favouring primates over non-primates, singling them out for special protection because of their species membership, could count as a form of speciesism. (Gary Francione has, in fact, advanced this charge as a reason to avoid singling out primates as a special object of concern.) However, Singer's position has always stuck close to familiar empirical realities of human domination. His tacit assumption is that the favoured species will be our own human species and the disadvantaged species will be non-human. And so, to all intents and purposes, speciesism of the sort which he attacked and continues to attack is a form of anthropocentric prejudice.

Identifying the prejudice in question as speciesism was a move which was geared to piggyback on concepts such as sexism and racism but it was not Singer who coined the term. Rather, it had become the common currency of **animal advocates** several years prior to the publication of *Animal Liberation* after being coined by Richard Ryder in 1970. As a clinical psychologist, Ryder had been a participant in animal experimentation but had then turned against the practice and went on to publish his own important exposé of experimental harms, *Victims of Science* (1975). The impact of the two texts marks out something interesting about subsequent patterns of influence. On the one hand, Singer became the best-known public face of animal advocacy (indeed, he is probably the best-known philosopher in the Western world). On the other hand, a series of quite different texts with less public impact had a more direct influence on the ideology of animal activists. (Here, the concept of 'ideology' is used in the neutral sense, as synonymous with some shared general outlook, rather than as an indication of the systematic misapprehension of the world.) Within two years of publication, Ryder was the chair of the RSPCA (Royal Society for the Prevention of Cruelty to Animals), the largest mainstream animal welfare charity in the UK, then at the height of its sympathies with an activist rights agenda. In this capacity, Ryder was able to call for a high-powered academic symposium on the Rights of Animals. The symposium, held at Trinity College, Cambridge, in 1977, was the single most important event in determining the shape of animal ethics for the remainder of the twentieth century. It brought together key academics (such as Tom Regan and Stephen Clark) and leading activists (such as Kim Stallwood) and it marked a close fusion between animal advocacy and a theory which was rights-based rather than focused, like Singer's position, on animal interests. The Trinity symposium produced a document on 'The Rights of Animals: A Declaration against Speciesism', whose signatories affirmed that '[w]e believe in the evolutionary and moral kinship of all animals and we declare that all sentient creatures have rights to life, liberty and the quest for happiness. We call for the protection of these rights.' Singer was, symbolically, absent. However, it may be interesting to speculate about the subsequent shape of the 'animal liberation' or 'animal rights' movement, had matters been otherwise. (The former term for organized animal advocacy is more sympathetic to Singer's position, the latter term is perhaps less so.)

The issue of rights has, over the course of time, become an important fracture line between Singer's position and the dominant outlook of organized animal advocates. Yet his account of the ethical standing of animals has nonetheless shaped an international animal advocacy movement which, from 1977 onwards, has become increasingly rights-focused. As we shall see, successive attempts to formulate a theory of animal rights have tended to involve reformulations of some of Singer's core arguments and commitments, and their translation into another terminology. However, there has been some hostility from those sections of the animal rights movement ('abolitionists') who argue that he does not go nearly far enough. (The concept of **abolitionism** will be explained in due course but readers with a special interest might go directly to Chapter 7.)

THE CORE OF SINGER'S POSITION

The approach set out in *Animal Liberation* and cashed out in more detail, and at a slightly more abstract level, in successive editions of Singer's *Practical Ethics* (1980, 1993, 2011), is broadly in line with liberal ethical and political norms. This can be seen in his commitment to variants of both liberty and equality. The liberalism which he puts into play involves commitment to a form of individualism, with Singer upholding the moral standing of the individual sentient being which has feelings and, in some cases, desires. This focus and the sidestepping of any direct consideration for communities and collectives is both characteristic of contemporary liberalism and is also one of its key claimed weaknesses. On such an outlook, appeals to animal communities, or to a human community, will carry no independent weight but must instead reduce to claims about the individual beings who happen to constitute the communities in question. This is a thoroughgoing liberalism.

Singer's account of equality is set up by appeal to an idea of universalizability as a test of ethical rules: if it is wrong for others to do something then it is also wrong for me to do it and vice versa. The same rules must apply equally to everyone. Nobody is privileged. Nobody is entitled to claim special standing as part of an elite, nobody is allowed to play the moral aristocrat. The rules which then apply to everyone are fixed by a commitment to utilitarian principles. The latter characteristically focus on minimizing harmful outcomes and maximizing the greatest good, or pleasure, or happiness or (in Singer's own case) preferences. Singer is what is known as a 'preference utilitarian'. This again allows his liberal egalitarianism to shine through. In contrast to some other, earlier and underconstrained versions of utilitarian theory, on Singer's account the ecstasy of the few cannot outweigh the sufferings of the many and the preferences of the latter *not* to suffer. It is not the total level of happiness, pleasure or preference satisfaction which matters, but rather the maximizing of preference satisfaction when constrained by an *equal* consideration of interests.

Utilitarians have often puzzled over whether or not to include the interests of animals within their calculations but this principle of the equal consideration of interests requires them to do so. There are, after all, no good grounds for excluding *any* sentient creature from consideration. Overall, what results is a form of **moral extensionism**, i.e. the identification of some or other reason why humans matter, followed by an argument that this will apply also in the case of at least some non-humans. However, Singer does not press the similarity of human and non-human further. What matters is not, for example, the possession of a specifically human-like awareness of the world, or a typically human capacity to engage in abstract reason. Rather, with regard to any creature whatsoever, what matters is not 'can they think?' but 'can they suffer?' Singer, here, is following directly in the footsteps of the utilitarian philosopher Jeremy Bentham, albeit he does so more consistently than the latter. (Bentham did not carry through this thought to any similarly sympathetic conclusion but instead supported **vivisection** in the furtherance of human interests. From Singer's standpoint, Bentham would have been a speciesist.)

Yet, even for a utilitarian, suffering, what constitutes suffering, and our attitude towards it, are no simple matters. Here, we might think of our varying reactions to visiting the dentist, or the willingness of some women to undergo childbirth on multiple occasions while others are deterred by the prospect of ever doing so. One option at this point is to imagine that we can simply partition and quantify all suffering into uniform and readily measurable units, descriptions of which can then function as data to be input into a calculus of pleasures and pains. (This is the classic and somewhat discredited utilitarian position initially advanced by Bentham.) Another option is to say (with John Stuart Mill) that how important any experience is, and what it is taken to involve, for a particular individual is best left to the individual to decide. This approach, of trying to maximize preferences or (more simply) choice, is again very much in line with our contemporary liberal understanding of exactly what is, ethically, most salient: the informed choices made freely by individuals themselves are given a privileged standing. However, in the case of creatures who cannot clearly articulate their preferences (or who might have none) we will in practice be guided by the familiar utilitarian consideration that, all other things being equal, it is desirable for individual creatures to experience pleasure and to avoid pain. And so, while Singer is officially a preference utilitarian, a good deal of his discussion of interests, in both *Animal Liberation* and *Practical Ethics*, is couched only indirectly in terms of preferences and more directly (also more simply) in terms of pleasure and pain. The necessary qualifier here is that claims about the latter are sometimes presumed to be shorthand for a more complex story. This, again, is one of Singer's strengths. He has always been prepared to streamline his position for the sake of impact.

What the argument, so far, blocks off is any reversion to the convenient view, influential during the formation of modern ethical theory in the 1600s and 1700s, that animal pain is not real pain but is merely a simulacrum or an outward behavioural show that lacks real inner substance. Such a view, often traced to the philosopher Descartes and to the idea of the mind as separate from the mechanical body, is no longer tenable (if it ever was). Our best evidence, and indeed our own familiar experience, suggests that a great many animals do feel pain, genuinely, intensely and, because of our human actions, frequently. As such, from Singer's point of view, they have interests which are due equal consideration to our own (my interests and yours too). We may still nonetheless wonder about whether this **moral considerability** of interest applies to *all* animals, and in particular to fish or insects as well as to cats, dogs, cows and pigs. But for Singer this is a matter which may be decided empirically. There is a good deal of evidence to suggest that fish do feel pain and Singer has endorsed the view that they do. Insects are, by contrast, a harder matter to speculate about. Even so, inclusion of such cases may make us wonder about exactly how far Singer's position can and ought to be pushed. Could the interests of either of these types of creatures conceivably have the same weight as that of a human, or a primate, or a richly sentient cat, dog or pig? We might be tempted to accept that he is right to argue for the moral considerability of animals, but be far less convinced that interests should be taken *equally* into consideration irrespective of their bearer. To say this is to accept that Singer may make a good case for the moral considerability of animals but that this on its own does not entail their equality with humans or with each other.

SPECIES EGALITARIANISM

Singer's case for a level of moral equality between humans and non-humans, rather than mere moral considerability, draws directly on our ways of thinking about moral equality between humans. Our acceptance of the latter does not depend on humans having exactly the same physiological characteristics, abilities or level of intelligence. If that were the case, humans would simply *not* enjoy moral equality with one another. Clever and slow-witted people would not each count as highly as the other. Yet, our presupposition is that they do. The former are not given priority access to organs for transplant, and the latter are not prevented from casting the single vote that each of us is entitled to. To uphold moral, and indeed political, equality among humans, we need to abandon any appeal to identical talents, skills, wisdom or insight. We need to abandon even the appeal to the possession of a special kind of rationality which humans simply do not all have to the same extent.

But once we suspend the idea that moral equality among humans can be underpinned by appeal to some uniform feature, there will be no reason to restrict the scope of equality *to* humans alone. Indeed, doing so could only involve an appeal to the one thing that all humans do share, i.e. our humanity. And any appeal to this, for Singer, seems perilously close to a form of prejudice, a bias which is based on an ethically irrelevant characteristic of *belonging to my group*. Yet the rejection of such bias does not automatically tell us what moral equality between humans and non-humans entails. According to Singer, it is best understood as a matter of having interests which are equally considerable. If I have an interest in avoiding the pain of an electrical shock, and a primate has an interest (to the same degree) in avoiding this same pain, then the mere fact that I am human does not entitle me to any special treatment. If we then go on to consider some other animal, a pig or a sheep, as long as it has the same pain-avoiding predicament to the same degree, there will be no good or defensible reason for considering its interest to be any less important than my own. This is Singer at his most radical, apparently levelling the standing of all sentient creatures, all creatures capable of having interests. My interests, your interests, and the interests of the dog in the street, are all *equally* worthy of consideration. But exactly how radical Singer really is becomes difficult to judge once some key qualifications to the position are drawn.

His position does not, for example, imply the abolition of all distinctions of importance, because individual creatures do not happen to have exactly the same sets of interests and those interests which they do happen to have in common are not always held to the same degree. If, for example, I have been partially desensitized to leg pain but you have not, then you will, in all likelihood (and all other things being equal), have a greater interest at stake when we encounter someone who wants to stick needles into our legs (unlikely though this may be). Similarly, but less in the manner of a thought experiment, most adult humans have a complex awareness of time and this opens up important possibilities for suffering guilt and experiencing fear through anticipation. It is a familiar point about humans that we (many or most of us) have ways of torturing ourselves that no other creature in existence happens to enjoy. Other animals experience fear and anxiety, but they do not worry about how they will put their children through college, how they are going to cope with their mortgage or whether they will still have a job in a year's time. Animals have no attitudes towards such matters. Similarly, they do not feel shame or guilt over an ill-chosen word. (They may, in some cases, experience shame or guilt over other things, but not over this.) This means that humans are often vulnerable to certain kinds of harm to which other animals are not vulnerable. And so, Singer's principle of equality is *not* that every animal and every human ought to be treated in exactly the same way all of the time (with an entitlement to vote, liability for fines, access to comparable diet and compulsory education) but *only* that equal consideration ought to be given to equal interests *where they exist*, and that this may lead, in practice, to very different forms of treatment for most humans and most non-humans.

In line with the above, if the interest that a particular animal has in retaining its territory is equal to that of a particular human in securing an education then there are no good grounds for prioritizing one over the other. But, by and large, it is likely that the trade-offs will favour humans. This is so because the capacity for our kind of rational deliberation (and all that goes with it) will tend to give the vast majority of humans a greater interest in the outcome of any particular decision. And this may make Singer's radicalism super-ficial rather than deep—a view which, right or wrong, has gained support within the animal rights movement (particularly so in the US). Singer has even gone so far as to argue that merely sentient creatures, who lack desires, do not have interests which are harmed by being killed, painlessly, in their sleep, because such interests would require them to have preferences concerning their future. The overall balance of utility would not be adversely affected if they were replaced by other merely sentient creatures of the same type. (Matters are very different with sentients, who are capable of desire-formation. They cannot be replaced without some failure to satisfy future-oriented desires.) But while this does seem to follow from a strict application of preference utilitarianism, such a conclusion might lead an animal advocate to say 'so much the worse for the theory'.

Some critics have levelled the charge that Singer is trapped inside an approach which captures only some aspects of the ethics of animal harm. And for strict opponents of animal slaughter, there has been an alarming drift in his writings towards acceptance that some kinds of ethically informed slaughter *might* be ethically permissible, at least in theory. However, there is danger here of amplifying marginal features of Singer's position at the expense of the core of what he has to say. Yet there are those (Jacques Derrida being the most obvious) who insist that what goes on at the margins of a position can tell us a great deal about what it finds most difficult to handle. Singer's problematic concessions in the case of mere sentients (whichever animals they may turn out to be) may also lead us to wonder about the depth of his commitment to any genuine and robust form of human/animal equality. It may then be useful to introduce a distinction between **weak species egalitarianism** of the sort that Singer subscribes to (and which in practice often favours humans) and **strong species egalitarianism** (which, even in practice, has no such human-favouring tendency).

It does, however, seem that both have the capacity to strike deeply at our sense of human superiority, at our sense of having a greater claim simply because we are humans without any need to have recourse to other considerations. It may seem to those who do not have any prior and strong ethical commitment to the value of animals that, once he reaches this point, Singer has already gone too far. In line with such a criticism, we may be inclined to revisit the whole issue of human difference and to ask why, in spite of the latter, we do embrace the equal consideration of human interests. The answer to this should, perhaps, be obvious but can be obscured if we focus our questioning on comparisons between individuals. Indeed, the persistent tendency to embrace a liberal focus on the individual may lead us to miss the obvious fact that we live in communities where ethics does not just answer to individual needs but also to social dangers. Abstracting from human difference and embracing the equal consideration of human interests is a way of doing just this. It may even be the only way in which we can hold a number of important social dangers in check. After all, we know from our history and, more specifically, from the worst aspects of our history, that inequality can and sometimes does lead to dreadful and unjustifiable harms. There may be no way to avoid the latter without rejecting the former. Considered at a society level, which in turn feeds through into the treatment of individuals, certain kinds of inequality may be bad all round, or at least bad overall. And for anyone who focuses on the overall consequences of our attitudes and actions, anyone who has at least some utilitarian inclinations, this may be decisive. Our intraspecies differences must, therefore, be set aside when considering the importance of one human by comparison with another. Equal consideration of interests across species, and in spite of huge variations in capacities, not just between humans and non-humans, but between different sorts of animals, may not have quite the same, clear, pragmatic justification.

By contrast, a refusal to embrace a principle of interspecies equality certainly does result in harms but not necessarily harms which any reasonable person would regard as utterly indefensible. And perhaps it is only those who are already convinced of the moral standing of animals who are likely to regard the consequences of moral inequality as utterly unacceptable. Accordingly, a critic of Singer's species egalitarianism may contend that there is a significant difference between the human case (where equality is pragmatically required) and the animal case (where equality would have to be justified by something other than an appeal to pragmatism). And so, a critic of Singer might argue that even his weak species egalitarianism could not, or should not, be adopted. The force of this 'could not' is that of an appeal to our intuitions. It is, in a sense, an appeal to utter incredulity at the idea that we could ever, genuinely, regard animals as our moral equals even in a qualified sense. Perhaps someone who leads a special kind of spiritual life, St Francis of Assisi or Buddha, could do so, or a Buddhist or Jain who is prepared to offer their body so that a tiger might eat, might do so, or someone living in a cloistered, academic world insulated from the give and take of ordinary human existence might do so. But a life lived ordinarily, in the midst of others, may seem to require us to be more discriminating.

A familiar exemplar to establish the point is the child-in-a-cage scenario, an example drawn from Cora Diamond but also used by Raimond Gaita. Suppose, while driving along, we were to look across at the vehicle beside us and see an animal in a cage. Perhaps we might feel that the animal ought not to be treated in this way. That it is wrong, or even very wrong. But would we feel just the same if, instead, we saw a human infant in the cage? *Could* we even do so without being in the grip of some peculiar ideology or psychological condition? *Actually* having the same responsive attitude towards humans and non-humans may be less attainable than we might imagine. Perhaps even exceptional individuals of the sort mentioned above could not be true egalitarians. There are, after all, limits to our moral psychology, to our value-laden ways of seeing and responding, and a truly egalitarian response may strain against these limits. Singer's own qualifications to his position, qualifications which allow humans to come out on top most of the time (because they usually have a greater interest at stake), might even be regarded as a clever or covert way of acknowledging a sense of practicality about such matters. He may then seem to be in the business of appropriating a weighty imagery and the appearance of a liberal egalitarianism which neither his theory nor common sense can support.

Set in more familiar philosophical terms, what is appealed to in such a criticism of species egalitarianism as inaccessible, or ultimately unavailable, is not just our intuitions but our *deepest* intuitions. Yet, while intuitions may be indispensable in ethics, they are not beyond challenge. Racism was once common sense and equality across racial groups (or what were perceived to be racial groups, given that the concept of race may be suspect) was deeply counter-intuitive, to the point of seeming utterly ridiculous. Even the ending of slavery in the US and the rise of ethico-political equality—up to full citizenship and equality before the law—were *not* at all taken to go hand in hand by the architects of emancipation. It took the devastation of war to shift matters in this direction. And while it is true that every great change has broken with established precedents and with deeply rooted intuitions, it is simply not true that there is a first time for everything or that every intuition is open to revision. Some changes simply do not occur. Utopian literature is full of examples of things which have not, and probably never will, come to pass.

And this is a point about the limits of *both* human psychology and social organization. They may each be malleable, but not infinitely so. A concern for a supporter of Singer, or for an advocate of any successor theory, is that species egalitarianism of whatever strength may press against these limits.

And even if we do accept that species egalitarianism of some kind is an available standpoint—one which could be embraced by individuals, even non-exceptional individuals and by society as a whole—the idea that society at large *ought* to embrace it may be less obvious. Once more, the critic of Singer can respond with a sense of sheer incredulity at the prospect of anyone responding identically to the plight of a human infant and to that of a dog. The suggestion that, when emotional limitations are set aside, this is the right way to respond, might be classified as what Raimond Gaita has (unflatteringly) called a 'fearless thought'. The very fact that an ethical position is so radically counter-intuitive or has such radically counter-intuitive implications *by itself* can give us reasonable grounds to suspect that it must be mistaken. Most positions of this sort do, after all, turn out to be false. Consider the claim that a defence of paedophilia is a defence of sexual freedom, or the claim that it is better not to bring any more humans into existence, or the claim that compulsory sterilization is the best answer to human overpopulation. All are fearless thoughts, and all are (by familiar and plausible standards) wildly wrong. If a position involves or leads to a conclusion which is so counter-intuitive that it seems patently absurd then the position may be deemed to be self-undermining. In the technical jargon of philosophical argument, the unpacking of an unacceptable, apparently false, conclusion functions as a *reductio ad absurdum* of the position in question. We might, in line with considerations of this sort, assume that somewhere in the reasoning which has led Singer to embrace even a weakened form of species egalitarianism, there simply must be a mistake. Something of this sort is a familiar response to encountering Singer's arguments for the first time while being unable to see where exactly he has gone wrong.

Let us suppose that there is something to this point. Let us allow that we do have reasons to be generally suspicious about or mistrustful of all or many fearless thoughts. And perhaps the idea of the equal consideration of interests across species really is an instance of such a thought. This still only gives us a methodological rule of thumb. It does not actually mean that such thoughts are always mistaken and it still does not mean that this particular fearless thought, concerning animals and equality, is mistaken. So how then should we proceed? Should we always stick with suspicion about any radical new idea, as a matter of methodological good sense? Such an approach might seem to be overly conservative. Perhaps, instead, even fearless thoughts ought not to be rejected as a matter of course if there is some further, countervailing consideration which may lead us to suspect that our existing intuitions, although deeply embedded, really are flawed. In the present case, when the claim of equality is made, there is at least one further consideration to which appeal might be made: we humans have an exceptionally poor track record of prejudicial attitudes and intuitions towards those who do not belong to our own limited group. Acceptance of this much is simply the acknowledgement of a good deal of empirical evidence. Arguing along these lines, Singer points out that, in the future, our attitude towards animals may be regarded as no less prejudiced than the historic attitudes which we now castigate as wildly wrong. This appeal to the future is, of course, conjectural, but it effectively draws attention to just how poor our track record happens to be. Perhaps, then, it is true that, as a methodological precaution, we ought to be cautious about fearless thoughts, but as a basic ethical precaution we may have good grounds for suspicions about our deep-seated human tendency towards bias. If grounds for ethical precaution trump merely methodological considerations then perhaps we should, on this matter, remain open to the possibility that it is our discriminating intuitions, and *not* the counter-intuitive egalitarian theory, which are at fault. And if this is the case, then an appeal to incredulity about either weak or strong species egalitarianism will not be an adequate response.

THE ECO-OBJECTION TO SENTIENTISM

Appeals to incredulity at the very idea that we can and should consider the interests of humans and other creatures equally, are consistent with an acceptance that animals do have at least some moral standing. But they also suggest that Singer has gone too far by moving from moral considerability to equal considerability (however qualified). Yet there is a different kind of objection to Singer's brand of species egalitarianism, an ecologically based objection which holds that he is quite right to challenge our belief in human supremacy, but he does not go far enough. The interests which figure in Singer's account of moral equality concern pleasure, pain and preference satisfaction. This makes them ultimately related to sentience and so it establishes a new form of priority and exclusion: the living but non-sentient, as well as the inanimate, are uniformly downgraded in favour of the sentient. And what this means is that while we might have duties which concern trees and rivers, such duties are indirect. That is to say, they are not really about the trees and rivers themselves. Instead, we have these duties because we also have direct duties towards sentient life forms and the latter depend on trees and rivers for their survival and well-being. To some ecologists, this appears to involve a form of prejudice which (like speciesism) is analogous to racism, sexism and anti-Semitism. The prejudice in question is generally referred to as **sentientism**. For ecological critics of Singer, such as advocates of an outlook known as Deep Ecology, in order to respond to *all* that is genuinely morally considerable we need to abandon Singer's restriction of interests to the interests of sentients. Instead, we need to extend considerability (even *equal* considerability, according to some of the earlier formulations of Deep Ecology) to forests, valleys, mountains and ecosystems which are not individual life forms but rather complexes of mutually related things, only some of which may happen to be biological organisms. The latter criticism veers clearly away from a liberal pattern of valuing towards a more holistic, communitarian or, perhaps more disturbingly, collectivist attitude. In response, the objections raised above against Singer—appeals to the radically counter-intuitive nature of his position—can now be adapted and run in Singer's defence. Animal advocates who are dedicated to liberal norms, to a valuing of the individual, can make their own appeal to incredulity about the valuing of non-sentients. (Although this leaves a good deal more to be said about a broader, claimed tension between animal advocacy and ecology.)

THE ARGUMENT FROM MARGINAL CASES

Often we tend to assume that the reason why the interests of humans simply must trump those of animals is that we have special, distinctively human and morally salient properties, such as self-consciousness and the capacity to reason, to use language and to form complex desires—properties that animals lack, or at least that they have only to a far lesser degree. And perhaps it would be the case that talk about the special importance of humans would be able to withstand Singer's charge of species prejudice if it were read as a form of shorthand for talk about these ethically salient differences between *us* and *them*.

The problem for Singer's critics is that this applies only up to a point. Whatever property, capacity, trait or cluster of traits we happen to think of as especially important will be possessed by at least some humans and some non-humans to the same extent or else it will be enjoyed to a greater extent by the latter rather than the former. Accordingly, if the possession of such traits is what makes humans important then it seems that some non-humans must be at least as important and perhaps even more so. Similarly, if we justify animal slaughter or animal experimentation, or any other such practice, by appeal to the limited cognitive capacities of these animals, we should then regard the very same practices as permissible in the case of all and any humans who happen to have similar traits or capacities. Humans such as infants and advanced dementia sufferers will be good candidates. If we are not prepared to sanction such practices in their case then we should not do so in the case of comparably equipped animals.

And so, if we want to justifiably exempt all and every human (including the 'marginal cases', such as infants and people with advanced dementia) from slaughter, involuntary experimentation and the full range of treatments to which we subject animals, we will then need to extend the very same level of protection to a wide range of animals. More generally, *if* it is wrong to treat any human in a particular way because they have some morally salient property *x*, *then* it is wrong to treat any animal in that way when they also have the same property *x*, or some comparable property, to the same extent.

This is known as the **argument from marginal cases** and early variants can be traced back to Porphyry in the third century CE. Although it has undergone a variety of reformulations, it has remained the core argument of animal advocates since the publication of *Animal Liberation*. The challenge to Singer's position from rival animal advocates, such as the rights theorists Tom Regan and Gary

Francione, has tended to be over other matters or else it has involved issues of reformulation rather than rejection. More specifically, a distinction has been drawn between Singer's *conditional* formulation of the argument and a more *categorical* formulation. Singer's version is conditional in the sense that it is couched in terms of an initial *if*. He does not say: *Because* humans with property *x* are protected, non-humans with this same property ought also to be protected. Rather, he says: *if* humans with property *x* are protected *then* non-humans with this same property ought to be protected. As an advocate of utilitarianism, who champions whatever will yield the maximal outcome in line with applying the same set of ethical principles to all, Singer cannot adopt any stronger and less conditional formulation. He cannot easily rule anything out. He might be able to do so if he were to adopt a version of utilitarianism which did generate some special absolute prohibitions, but such a version of utilitarianism would look suspiciously like a disguised account of rights theory.

The upshot is that Singer's conditional formulation of the argument has been strongly criticized by animal advocates who do want a more definite exclusion of harms to beings (both human and animal). It has also been criticized by defenders of a traditional Christian conception of morality who detect, in the argument's detail, a devaluation of the human which might sanction dreadful harms. These problems arise for Singer because his version of the argument is essentially a criticism of inconsistency. We claim to be protecting humans *because of* their special properties, and when we find out that some other creature has the same properties we want to change the game and to apply a new and different set of rules. But while the inconsistency can be resolved by protecting animals (which is clearly Singer's favoured outcome) it can also be resolved by removing protection from certain classes of impaired or infantile humans. And this is just what many commentators fear. By contrast with a levelling-up of the standing of animals, there can be a levelling-down of the standing of a large number of humans. Concern with this, and with the difficulties which Singer faces if he wishes to exclude such a possibility, has resulted in the targeting not just of his argument, but also (albeit occasionally) of his public lectures and institutional affiliations. The argument has made him a controversial figure to be associated with.

OBJECTIONS TO THE ARGUMENT FROM MARGINAL CASES

Perhaps surprisingly, in the light of the amount of scrutiny to which it has been subjected, the argument from marginal cases has turned out to be unusually resilient in the face of a variety of criticisms. Two, in particular, stand out: firstly, the objection that there must be some hidden human uniqueness which Singer and others have simply failed to spot; and secondly, the claim that what matters in terms of ethical standing is not actually the properties of any individual creature but, rather, the average or normal properties of the group (or species) to which the creature belongs.

A major difficulty for the first of these criticisms is that whether or not such a universally and exclusively human property can be identified, this line of argument is in danger of proving too much. Suppose, for example, that we were to encounter a species with some remarkable and universally shared property which we terrestrial humans all happen to lack or have only to a lesser degree. Perhaps, they might have some sort of super-reason. Would this make the members of that species entitled to dominate us in the way that we dominate non-humans? Would it make them entitled to enslave us, breed us and kill us for their sport? Would their lives and interests matter more than ours do? Many of us will be inclined to say that such a property could not underpin such claims of human inferiority. Others might concede that it would depend on the nature of the property in question. Yet it is difficult to see why this would matter. Why would we think that even such remarkable intellectual powers granted superior moral standing? After all, to repeat a point which has already been made by Singer, we simply do not grade the value of humans, and the relative importance of their interests, by how clever they are. Any such consideration is utterly irrelevant to judgements about who matters and about exactly how much they matter. The obvious thought then is that once a certain threshold for reasoning skills has been reached (our threshold) all creatures at or above the threshold are equal. But this seems arbitrary, and it does not address the very issue that the argument from marginal cases draws attention to: there will always be some humans, the 'marginal-case' humans, who fall below *any* given threshold. And, in spite of this, we will still be reluctant to strip them of their high moral standing.

If some property were ever to be identified, a property which did mark a difference in all cases when we compare humans and non-humans, this would also have to be a property which is very closely linked to being human. The options for such a property are limited. One possibility, which is currently out of favour but which has historically helped to shape the domination of animals, is that we are in possession of an immortal soul or that we have the property of being loved by God or being chosen by him for dominion over other creatures. Given the extent to which religious outlooks continue to shape our lives, this cannot be set aside as a simple appeal to falsehood. It may well be a coded way of saying something deeper and more complex. It may also be, for many people, a last line of defence for the uniqueness of the human. Indeed, for certain kinds of religious agent it may be a striking affirmation of their faith that strictly secular, even scientific, accounts of what it is to be human, cannot explain why it is that we are so special. Yet such talk faces a pragmatic difficulty. It is not a justification for human superiority which all reasonable agents will feel compelled to accept. Indeed, many of us will claim that it is simply false, or that talk about having souls and about creation may be instructive mythologies or figurative ways of speaking, but they do not belong within this kind of discussion. Rather, they are at home within discussions of how we should love rather than discussions of who we imagine ourselves superior to. When it comes to the shaping of public policy about slaughter, animal experimentation and basic interests, a spiritually neutral way of addressing matters may be appropriate. Perhaps, religious claims should still have a place in the discussion but only insofar as they are translatable into something else which can command a wider assent. And once such a translation is made we are back to square one and the specialness of the human again seems mysterious.

Alternatively, instead of looking to religion we could look to science and point out that *all* of us have human DNA while no other creature does. That, surely, is an ethically salient matter although, here, the strength of our conviction that this is important might be weakened by reflection that our DNA is mostly the same as non-human DNA. We share about 36 per cent of our DNA with fruit flies, 15 per cent with mustard grass, 85 per cent with zebra fish and 98 per cent with chimpanzees. (And we certainly do not treat fruit flies 36 per cent as well as we treat humans or accord chimpanzees

98 per cent of our human rights.) In any case, the DNA which is ours is possessed in only about 10 per cent of the cells which make up our bodies. We are vastly outnumbered, from the outset, by other life forms with whom we have symbiotic, or hostile, relations. In sheer bodily terms, *we* are mostly *them*. But even if we were to convince ourselves that differences of DNA could be important, what we would then have might look suspiciously like a form of code fetishism. Why would we think that our genetic code itself *in its own right* matters at all? Of course it matters a great deal in terms of what it codes for. It matters instrumentally because of what it can bring about. But this is rather different from saying that the code itself carries some special, **intrinsic value** all of its own. Suppose, for example, that I had a different code which was able to function and operate in the same way, one which was packed into a triple helix, or which had five base units instead of four. This would make me an interesting sort of research subject, but would it make me more or less important than others, or the bearer of greater or lesser interests? Again, suppose that we happen to meet creatures from elsewhere in the universe who have very different DNA or no DNA at all but, instead, some different information-packing and reproducing system. It would be a dreadful conceit to imagine that this alone could make any difference to their moral standing.

Be that as it may, the main difficulty for Singer and other advocates of the argument from marginal cases is that while the argument carries an insight, once people accept that there simply is no special human property they often tend to think that it is mildly inconvenient but that, ultimately, it does not matter. Instead, the critic of Singer can fall back on the claim that humans are humans and other creatures are not. In a sense this is a property, but it is not a special property which is set apart from our humanity itself. The tangible property which humans have in common, and which all animals lack, simply is our humanity. Michael Pollan, a popular critic of Singer, in his best-selling *The Omnivore's Dilemma* (2006), is drawn towards just this point. Being human is itself taken to be ethically salient. This view can, again, be presented as a strictly secular claim or as a religious claim of a more subtle sort, the claim which Christian religious discourse presents in an indirect form. Indeed, a great deal of religious discourse about God's love for mankind, for all of us no matter who we are, what we are like or what we have done, can be cashed out as a figurative way to make sense of the idea that *being human*, on its own, is enough to make us equally and distinctively valuable. In line with this, perhaps we should never have allowed Singer to set aside the idea that an appeal to our species membership must reduce to a form of prejudice.

Problematically, at least if this position is cast in anything like Pollan's terms, this does look suspiciously like a form of 'speciesism', an otherwise unreasoned prejudice in favour of 'our own'. After all, exactly the same argument could be run in favour of racial prejudice (what all white people have, and others do not have, is their whiteness); sexism (what all men have, and women lack, is their manhood); or anti-Semitism (what all Gentiles have, and Jews lack, is the fact that they are Gentiles and not Jews). While species membership is clearly important when it comes to determining appropriate nutrition, biological structure, mating possibilities and similar matters, it remains difficult to understand exactly why it would support any claim that our interests are of a different order, or that they are greater or lesser than those of other beings. The very idea of human superiority really does seem to be a social construct, a conceit which is not at all built into the nature of things. It would be very odd to try and maintain it if we ever did encounter a group of cultured but non-human beings. Yet this consideration leaves us in some difficulty. It now starts to look as if Singer may be correct and that there really is no ethically salient property that all humans have to a greater degree than all animals.

This will still leave us with the second dominant line of attack: an appeal to normal or average capabilities as standard setting. Singer's formulation of the argument from marginal cases seems resilient while we abide by the rules of liberal individualism and judge matters on a case-by-case basis: if we have no entitlement to do something to a human with property x, because they have property x, then we will have no entitlement to do that same thing to a non-human with some comparable property. But what if we suspend our focus on the individual and portion out moral standing in line with the average capabilities of species? Tibor Machan argues precisely this: we should base our assessment of individual cases on the average species capabilities rather than the particularities of the individual. We will then have clear grounds for preserving the special entitlements of even the most 'marginal' of humans while excluding comparably equipped and capable animals from the same entitlements. And here, the argument benefits from appeal to a fact which is not at all in dispute: overall, humans generally do have competences and properties that non-humans mostly lack to a comparable degree. Machan seems to be appealing to the very consideration which does, ordinarily, help to shape our appraisal of matters, rather than having to appeal to anything more abstract and theory-laden (such as a special claim drawn from religion or science).

While this does have the virtue of helping to make sense of our familiarly established practice, it does exactly what Jacques Derrida and various continental thinkers have identified as a key failing of certain kinds of Western philosophical thought: it embraces a wilful blindness to difference (a failing alleged to be at the heart of a number of ethical problems). Moreover, why should we say that the average capabilities of a species are what matters rather than the average capabilities of some other kind of grouping such as sentient creatures (as opposed to non-sentient creatures) or of mammals as opposed to reptiles? Or why not appeal to the average capabilities of primates (which would include humans)? The latter moves will, in each case, put humans down on all fours with a great many other creatures who happen to belong also to the same group. Even if we do opt for a group-average approach, there seems to be no compelling reason, other than a desire to fix the outcome in advance, to identify species as the relevant group-level unit. There is, then, at least the danger of circularity if it turns out that the appeal to average group capabilities requires us to already assume that, out of all the available group boundaries, species boundaries are precisely the ones which matter.

If this is not enough to cast doubt on such an appeal, there is a further consideration which might do so and which might lead us to acknowledge that the particularity of individual creatures simply cannot be ignored. Against the average approach, the novelist J. M. Coetzee has appealed to a short story by Franz Kafka in which a fictionally intelligent ape, Red Peter, gives an address to a learned academy. The address is urbane, witty and even erudite. Everything is in place for Red Peter's acceptance as a fellow scholar except his species membership. Should such a creature be denied access to a university, or to scholarly recognition or to anything at all which a comparably erudite and sophisticated human would be entitled? To press for such exclusion would seem to spill over from a reasonable group appraisal, about what is often the case, into a form of injustice based on stereotyping. It would, above all, be difficult to justify such actions to Red Peter himself without having to apologize for the policy. And what if Red Peter (like the fictional *other creatures* mentioned above) was smarter than we are? Should we still be given preference for a teaching post because what matters are average capabilities? That would seem distinctly odd, and uncomfortably close to the view that Red Peter should lose out because (in terms made famous, not by Coetzee, but by a well-known film) he is just a 'damned, stinking ape'.

CONCLUSION

Singer's position is both distinctive and set apart from the lines of division which have emerged between supporters of animal rights and defenders of an ethically informed continuation of our domination and control over non-humans. For the latter, he goes too far, with ideas of an equal consideration of interests—a form of what I have called weak species egalitarianism. For at least some of the former, he does not go far enough. Any rights theorist who wants a strict exclusion of animal harms, rather than an evaluation of whether or not they maximize preference satisfaction, will hold that too many concessions are made and that what is required will be closer to a strong species egalitarianism—although what this will look like is, as yet, unclear. And for all manner of critics (animal advocates as well as opponents of animal rights) his way of treating our humanity as an ethically irrelevant consideration may seem difficult to accept. Although, again, to recognize this is very different from identifying what (if anything) such a discounting of our humanity happens to miss.

FURTHER READING

Singer's core texts on animal ethics are *Animal Liberation* (London: Random House, 1995 [1975]), *Practical Ethics* (New York: Cambridge University Press, 2011 [1980, 1993]), and (with Jim Mason) *The Ethics of What We Eat* (Emmaus, PA: Rodale, 2006).

For the concept of 'speciesism' see Tony Milligan, 'Speciesism as a Variety of Anthropocentrism', in Rob Boddice (ed.), *Anthropocentrism* (Boston and Leiden: Brill, 2011); and for an alternative approach which attempts to implicate Singer in this prejudice, Joan Dunayer, *Speciesism* (Derwood, MD: Ryce Publishing, 2004).

For a critique of Singer for going too far in his sympathies for animals, see Tibor Machan's *Putting Humans First: Why We Are Nature's Favorite* (Lanham: Rowman & Littlefield, 2004). For ecological criticisms of Singer's individualism see Patrick Curry, *Ecological Ethics* (Cambridge: Polity Press, 2011).

3

REGAN ON ANIMAL RIGHTS

To say that *if* we cannot treat any human in a particular way *then* we cannot treat animals with comparable properties in that way seems to leave open the possibility that both humans and animals might be treated in the manner in question. From a **utilitarian** point of view, if it happened to generate the greatest well-being, then both might legitimately be used for the greater good, irrespective of their own desires, wishes or well-being. The difficulty here is not one of incautious formulation, but rather it is a problem of utilitarianism as such. As a theory, it seems unable to offer sufficient protection to individuals. It is, of course, possible to take protective steps by adding principles or rules which do try to offer guarantees to the individual in the face of any calculation about the greater good. But any version of utilitarianism which is sufficiently stringent in its deployment of such rules and principles will no longer look like a genuine instance of utilitarianism. Instead, it will begin to resemble a version of rights theory. Because of the greater protection afforded by the latter, it has been the dominant position among **animal advocates** since an early point in the development of the animal liberation movement. For most animal advocates associated with this movement, rights rather than utilitarian calculations about interests need to be at the heart of any critique of **speciesism** or, more simply, human dominance.

Animal rights theory has, in turn, been dominated by two main figures: Tom Regan, who first presented an early, and very scholarly, philosophical defence of animal rights in the late 1970s, and Gary Francione, whose work dates from the 1990s onwards and is more polemical (also more accessible). Francione's position is explored in Chapter 7 and is, in some respects, a modification of Regan, just as Regan's position emerged as a modification of Singer. For Regan, what matters ethically is not, primarily, the maximizing of outcomes but rather the performance of duty, together with respect for the standing and value of others (non-humans as well as humans). Outcomes do matter on this approach, as they need to on any plausible approach, but the pursuit of any given outcome must involve respect for duty and for rights-bearers. Accordingly, it may be important (outcome maximizing) for us to find out various sorts of information or acquire various kinds of knowledge, but we cannot torture others or subject them to extreme involuntary harms in order to do so. Armed with this approach, in his main text, *The Case for Animal Rights* (1983), Regan shifts the case for animal advocacy from Singer's conditional or hypothetical formulation of the **argument from marginal cases** towards a categorical and more restrictive formulation: *given that there are actions which we are not allowed to perform on any human we should conclude that we are also not allowed to perform those same actions on animals who have comparable moral properties.*

This removes the open-endedness of Singer's position which critics have found objectionable. By virtue of being restrictive, and basing itself on an appeal to rights, Regan's position is also more closely aligned to the standpoint of the majority of animal advocates and it is particularly close to the standpoint of the activists who engage in public protests, agitation and illegal actions such as the rescue of animals from laboratories and from the food industry. But his position is also rather more complex and deductive, more rigorously thought out and academically oriented. It is shaped not only by a conception of what animals are due, but also by a conception of what a good philosophical ethic should look like. This can make the details of what he has to say rather difficult to access. The upshot is that Regan's commitment to rights has influenced activism, shaped and reinforced the dominance of a rights-based approach, but without ever managing to displace Singer, whose considerable impact on animal advocacy continues in both direct and indirect forms. It continues directly, through the endorsement by animal advocates, of many individual claims and arguments which his writings advance. And it continues indirectly, through critique. It is, above all, Singer, who is the target of the most widely read, ethically informed defences of meat-eating, for example by Michael Pollan.

This also means that when trying to make sense of Regan, a greater degree of caution is required than might otherwise be the case. It often makes sense to differentiate between the position which someone advances and the *uptake* of that position by others, i.e. the way it is read and what is credited to the author. This is especially so with Regan. What complicates matters is a tendency to see the most important texts of both Singer and Regan in the light of subsequent arguments. One of the major influences on the contemporary animal rights movement is an approach now known as **abolitionism**, typified by Gary Francione's second-generation challenge to the apparently more moderate first-generation Singer and Regan approaches. Singer and, as we shall see, Regan also, advocates a **weak species egalitarianism**. Francione's position looks far closer to **strong species egalitarianism**. Yet **abolitionist** critiques of those deemed, by Francione and others, to have failed to go far enough, have tended to be more conciliatory towards Regan than towards Singer. This dovetails with the fact that while Singer has tended to emphasize the proximity between his position and Regan's, the latter has increasingly tended to emphasize those matters on which they are in disagreement. Over time, the idea of their radical divergence has taken hold. And so, while first-wave activists (of the 1970s and especially the early 1980s) tended to regard Singer and Regan as making a similar case in different ways, second-wave activists (of the 1990s and early 2000s) have tended to see the two as much further apart.

SUBJECTS-OF-A-LIFE

One thing which has remained constant throughout Regan's presentation of his position is an insistence on the central importance of what he calls **subjects-of-a-life**. These are inherently valuable beings whose standing must be respected and given its due. They are beings towards whom we have duties. This focus on beings, and the kind of beings who clearly matter, is a persistent theme. And so, for Regan, one of the key problems with Singer's approach is that the focus of equality is on interests rather than on the equality of beings themselves. It is, for Singer, interests which are equally considerable. And while we might suspect that this is just a different way of saying what Regan wants to say, he does not believe that this is the case. He suggests that Singer holds a 'receptacle' account of beings and value: humans and animals can have valuable things *in* them (the right kind of experiences, those which are connected to the satisfaction of their preferences) or they can fail to do so, but it is the contents rather than the container which is deemed to be ultimately of value. Any notion that humans or animals are inherently valuable beings *in their own right* seems to drop out of this picture.

As a matter of justice towards Singer, Regan is *not* disputing the point that experiences and preference satisfaction matter, in the sense that they are important for some or other creature or creatures. Indeed, he is ready to affirm that Singer is quite right to consider experiences as important and also to cash out their importance in terms of preferences rather than by appeal to the raw feel of the experiences themselves. For Regan, experiences can be intrinsically valuable in the sense that they are desired or desirable for their own sake and not for the sake of something else. But the **intrinsic value** of such experiences is not to be confused with the, ethically more important, **inherent value** of beings, and more especially those who are subjects-of-a-life, i.e. creature capable of experiencing and forming attitudes towards the world. More specifically,

> [i]ndividuals are subjects-of-a-life if they have beliefs and desires; perception, memory, and a sense of the future, including their own future; an emotional life together with feelings of pleasure and pain; preference and welfare-interests; the ability to initiate action in pursuit of their desires and goals; a psychophysical identity over time; and an individual welfare in the sense that their experiential life fares well or ill for them, logically independently of their utility for others and logically independently of their being the object of anyone else's interests.

It is not entirely clear whether Regan intends this list of characteristics as, in each instance, a necessary requirement, or rather as part of a cluster which needs to be satisfied only broadly or for the most part. A relatively open attitude towards who might qualify suggests that it is not intended to be read in the more restrictive manner. On Regan's understanding, all humans, except those in an irreversible coma or in a permanent vegetative state, will qualify. This applies even to children and to the mentally impaired. All will have inherent value and the rights which go with being of such value. What this means is that **moral patients** (sentient beings who cannot decide and act for themselves) as well as **moral agents** (sentient beings who can both decide and act) will both qualify. They will both be rights-bearers. And once moral patients qualify, it is clear that a great many animals (mammals especially) must also do so, except on some peculiar underestimation of their capacities.

Yet, in spite of its inclusiveness, Regan's approach is not *comprehensively* inclusive. Some creatures are not subjects-of-a-life. They lack the relevant agency and psychological cohesion. But exactly how many creatures are likely to be excluded, and which creatures are likely to be excluded (fish perhaps), is difficult to say prior to a case-by-case examination. By contrast, Singer's approach, generously understood or modified, looks as if it will generate moral standing for absolutely all sentient creatures irrespective of the kind of agents that they are.

However, this limitation is, at least partly, strategic. Regan presents his list of criteria for subjects-of-a-life as *sufficient* conditions for being morally considerable, and not as *necessary* conditions. He allows that other grounds for **moral considerability** may conceivably be added on. Overall, his argument aims to show that *at least* certain classes of animals are considerable in a way which involves their having rights. A conspicuous aspect of this approach is, however, that it seems to focus on precisely the same human-like considerations which ecologists have also found problematic in Singer's case. This, at least, is the way in which Regan has often been read by critical ecologists, as someone who is again pressing sentience as the basis of value and, as in Singer, only individual creatures can have sentience. Composites or 'systems' such as forests or ecosystems will still not have any standing in their own right unless some supplementary theory of value is tagged on. Instead, they will have only the aggregate standing of their individual components. What Regan then seems to provide is a different kind of liberal, individualist position from Singer, but it is still a position which is liberal, individualist and to the ecologically minded it is likely to seem insufficiently sensitive to holistic considerations.

INHERENT VALUE

A good deal of the contemporary literature on rights suggests that they are the result of embeddedness within a community through some form of contract. There is, however, an older tradition of rights discourse which attaches rights directly to individuals by virtue of their natural characteristics. One very traditional way of doing this is to say that humans are made in the image of God and that various entitlements go with this bounty. Regan's approach belongs very much within this natural rights tradition, albeit as a secular variant. He does, however, manage to avoid one of the familiar problems which has tended to beset natural rights theory: the requirement to shift from purely factual claims (about natural properties) to claims about value. This has left natural rights theory vulnerable to the charge that it illegitimately attempts to derive *ought* claims from *is* claims (a move which is sometimes known as the **naturalistic fallacy**—more cautiously, this is Regan's understanding of the latter, disputed concept).

Regan gets around the problem by appealing to consistency and to our *considered beliefs*, i.e. to our acceptance of ethical claims in the light of deliberation. He tries to understand what the claims in question require in order to be true. For example, in the case of inherent value, if two beings are considered to have equal inherent value then there must be at least some underlying natural features which they have in common. Similarly, if two beings do not have equal inherent value then there must be some underlying divergence in their natural features. They could not, for example, be identical twins while one was inherently valuable and the other was not. (This is, of course, very different from a relational approach which would allow for such a possibility.) Our best account of the value of humans will appeal to the fact that they have various underlying ethically salient properties. However, the precise connection between these properties and inherent value is left open-ended. (A popular move is to say that the ethical properties *supervene* on the natural properties, a move which then requires a complex theory of **supervenience**.) There is no deduction of the existence of inherent value from the existence of any particular natural properties but rather there is the identification of a correlation between the two in the agreed case of human subjects (or rather, human subjects-of-a-life). From this, we are licensed to say that the properties (those associated with being the subject-of-a-life) are a marker also for the inherent value of animals.

While Regan's commitment to rights has been embraced by animal advocates, there has been greater caution about any such account of inherent value. To some, it has seemed just too metaphysically obscure or even impolitic. Why go for a metaphysically deep and complex account of value, which is unlikely to secure the agreement of all reasonable agents, when the latter are more likely to acknowledge the obvious significance of interests? Indeed it is this very consideration which Singer cites in support of his own early decision to set aside all talk about rights. There is, however, a further option. There is the option of bringing these two concepts together by saying that to have a right with regard to something is simply to have an interest which is sufficiently strong to impose a duty on others. (We shall return to this interest-based approach to rights in Chapter 9.) This avoids metaphysical obscurity, appeals to what can readily command acceptance as a matter of importance, and thereby opens the way to democratic agreement about the ethical standing of animals, but it does so in a way which is quite different from Singer. It does not require us to buy into any utilitarian calculations which might lead to the sacrifice of individuals. It focuses on interests but it is nonetheless a rights discourse.

A further difficulty which faces Regan is that, like Singer, he *does* want to capture a commitment to egalitarianism, one which can match Singer's own insistence on the equal consideration of interests. But Regan does this by insisting that inherent value is absolute, it does not come in degrees. All creatures who have inherent value do so *to the same extent*, i.e. equally. However, the incredulity with which Singer's commitment to species egalitarianism has been met now carries over to Regan. It has seemed wildly implausible to those outside of the animal rights movement—implausible even to many animal advocates—that all creatures (from humans to mice) are, even at some ultimate level, of equivalent worth. Some critics, such as Mary Anne Warren (who also advances the charge of metaphysical obscurity against Regan), have suggested that the appeal to inherent value does not do the work that Regan wants it to do. Two reasons for this are offered. Firstly, even if animals did have inherent value it is difficult to see why this would automatically generate rights; and secondly, it is implausible to suggest that inherent value, should it exist, could not come in degrees. After all, there are very different ways of being the subject-of-a-life or, more simply, being sentient. By contrast, Warren favours a weaker conception of animal rights which does not appeal to any form of species egalitarianism. We may then wonder why someone like Warren might support a rights discourse at all. The answer to this is simple: appeals to considerations such as cruelty simply do not generate enough prohibitions. They leave it unclear why painless killing is ethically problematic. Sufficient prohibitions require a rights discourse to be at least part of an animal ethic. On this matter Warren holds that Regan has always been right. But such an ethic need not drape itself in the language of liberal equality.

RIGHTS AND PRINCIPLES

Although Regan opts for rights theory rather than consequentialism, like Singer, his approach also involves endorsement of a form of equality with the same rules applying equally to everyone. In other words, we do not get to make ethics up depending on the particularities of the situations in which we happen to find ourselves. In this respect, both Singer and Regan are strongly influenced by the tradition of Immanuel Kant, the eighteenth-century German philosopher who regarded ethics as a system of universally applicable principles, deducible in turn from one master principle which could be formulated in a variety of ways. In terms of their philosophical temperaments, they are no great distance from this view. Yet, as indicated in Chapter 1, this approach to ethics has been criticized because of its remoteness from the way in which we actually live our lives. However, it may be our uninformed and complacent practice which is at fault and not their more constrained approach towards being ethical.

Whereas Singer tries to pare matters back to a compact and easily understood set of considerations, a more complex sequence of inter-related principles is used by Regan to make sense of our predicament. This predicament involves having to choose, from time to time, between the interests of one inherently valuable subject-of-a-life and another. The first of these principles is the **respect principle** and it is (or at least seems) uncontroversial: creatures with inherent value are to be treated in ways which respect their inherent value.

This follows more or less automatically from the fact that there is such a thing as inherent value and it affirms the point that recognition of it ought to be action-guiding. Here, again, the terminology sticks very close to the tradition of Immanuel Kant, albeit Kant is well known for having restricted the requirement for respect in ways which make it a response only to autonomous rational agents, i.e. people like us. From the respect principle, Regan believes that it is possible to deduce the **harm principle**: we have a direct prima facie (on the face of things) duty not to harm individuals who have inherent value. Refraining from harm is itself a required way of respecting those creatures who have inherent value.

Two aspects of the harm principle do, however, require further explanation. Firstly, the duty not to harm is direct rather than indirect. This contrast (of direct and indirect) is again drawn from the Kantian tradition. Kant claimed that we have duties towards autonomous rational agents because of the importance which the latter have in their own right (they are 'ends in themselves'). By contrast, he argued that we have only indirect duties towards animals. We do have duties towards them, but only because our actions towards them might ultimately impinge on humans. For example, if our treatment of animals shapes our character in ways which make cruelty an option then this might ultimately spill over into our relations with other rational beings (in effect, humans). While Kant may have been trying to cash out the intuition that certain kinds of animal harm really are wrong, the way in which he did so suggested that it was not the animals themselves which are important. The standing that he gave to animals was, therefore, radically compromised. And this has, for a long time, been a source of unease about any application of Kantian ethics to non-humans. Regan solves the problem, while retaining a broadly Kantian standpoint and a good deal of Kant's conceptual machinery, by insisting that our duty to avoid harming individual animals, and our duty to avoid harming individual humans, are both direct duties. Indeed, they are aspects of the same single prima facie duty not to harm.

Secondly, the harm principle is, as stated, a prima facie matter. Regan is not advancing absolute pacifism or an ultimate religious taboo on harm. This is not an equivalent of the Buddhist, Hindu and Jain principle of ahimsa (we should not harm, no matter what, even though in a sense we cannot avoid harming). Rather, it is a default position that we should not harm individuals who have inherent value, but the default position can be overridden under suitable circumstances. This allows Regan's position to qualify as, up to a point, pragmatic. But our licence to harm is itself subject to constraint. More precisely, it is governed by two further principles which help to determine how and when the harm principle may be overridden. The first constraint is that, where overridden, it is to be overridden to the minimum viable extent. This idea is captured by the **miniride principle**: we should minimize overriding. In brief, it states that it is better to fail the few than to fail the many when we must fail one or the other. If, for example, I have some limited two-position control over a streetcar which cannot be stopped, I should channel it in the direction of a single individual rather than in the direction of a crowd (again, if I must choose one or the other). This will involve harm, but the least harm under the circumstances, and so it will involve the least violation of the principle that we should respect others by not harming them. However, even though this trade-off is acceptable, I am not allowed to go around harming individuals in the interests of some greater number of individuals when a trade-off is not forced on me. Figuratively, if there is no out-of-control streetcar then we should not set one going. This distinguishes the miniride approach from utilitarianism, or at least it aspires to do so.

The second constraint is the **worse-off principle**. If we must harm the innocent many or the innocent few (or one) there is a circumstance under which we are allowed to harm the many. Regan believes that this is again derivable from the requirement for respect. Let us suppose that my streetcar is speeding out of control and is about to hit either a single unprotected pedestrian or a heavily protected and well-prepared group of pedestrian stuntmen whose speciality is being hit by streetcars. They might be bruised by the process but I should still opt to harm them minimally rather than harm the single pedestrian greatly. More generally, if the harm to the few (or to the one) which would result from my actions is greater than the harm which would result to any of the many, then I am licensed to harm the many. What makes matters rather more complex is that the harms cannot be reduced to a single metric which might allow us to say that five harms of type x are equal to three harms of type y. We cannot fall back on any utilitarian calculus.

We may, nonetheless, wonder about the style of reasoning which is used to set up these constraints. It has been charged that, while there may be no utilitarian calculus of pains in Regan, there is nonetheless a clear slippage towards a consequentialist or utilitarian mode of deliberation. What results may not be utilitarianism of Singer's sort, but it does look suspiciously like utilitarianism of some sort. And it does give the impression that Singer may have been right all along to claim that the distance between his position and Regan's has been exaggerated. Indeed, now that we are allowed, under some circumstances, to harm individual subjects-of-a-life—just so long as we abide by the appropriate set of rules—we may begin to suspect that what is really respected is not the subject-of-a-life but rather the moral principles themselves. (This is a long-standing charge levelled at principle-based ethics and at **Kantianism** in particular.)

THE PROBLEM OF LIFEBOAT CASES

Regan's principles, and the worse-off principle in particular, have consequences which lead some commentators to question both his distance from Singer and the strength, depth or genuineness of his species egalitarianism. These two points are related. As with Singer, a species egalitarianism which allows humans to be favoured in practice, most of the time, is at best a version of weak species egalitarianism. Some may charge that it does not look like the real thing. The coalescing of their positions on this matter is, in part, a result of their agreement that harm is best understood in terms of preferences (i.e. desires) rather than understood directly in terms of painful experiences. The rationale for this is simple and powerful: if someone kills us painlessly while we are sleeping, we have still been harmed and the harm in question cannot be a matter of having painful experiences because there are none. Rather, it involves the curtailment of desire satisfaction and the prevention of various existing desires, such as a desire to do something later, from being realized.

Considerations of this sort help both Singer and Regan to insist that animal slaughter, no matter how it is carried out, involves harm just so long as the creatures in question are capable of having at least some future-oriented preferences. (Something which, as we have seen, Singer concedes, is not always the case.) But this breadth of criticism of slaughter comes at a price. Most humans and most animals share various desires for food, sex, shelter and (in the case of social animals) companionship and affection. But in addition, most humans also have a further set of desires concerning the future. Humans have desires to settle down, raise offspring, have successful careers and, in some cases, write books about ethics. The upshot is that the death of a human typically (not always but typically) involves a greater curtailment of desires and, hence, more harm, than the death of an animal. Singer and Regan are, again, in agreement on this point as are most supporters of desire-satisfaction accounts of well-being. Many do, however, add the qualification that what promotes well-being is the satisfaction of the right kind of desires rather than just any desires (a moralizing qualification to which Singer and Regan do not obviously subscribe).

The problem for Regan is that when it is combined with this approach, the worse-off principle starts to misbehave or at least it starts to yield results which may lead us to question the viability of species egalitarianism. Recognition of his difficulties emerged quickly, and very publicly, shortly after publication of *The Case for Animal Rights* in the form of a heated exchange between Singer and Regan in the *New York Review of Books*. The focus of the disagreement has been a recurring source of criticisms at which Regan has expressed some surprise. To explain the worse-off principle, he had set the seemingly straightforward example of 'the dog in a lifeboat'. Four humans and one dog are in a lifeboat under circumstances where there is one creature too many in the boat for survival. According to Regan, under most circumstances, where the humans are cognitively normal adults, innocent of any great crime and their shared predicament is not the fault of the humans to begin with, the right thing to do will be to throw the dog overboard because greater harm would accrue to any of the humans if they were thrown overboard. They would be made worse off than the dog by being drowned. This suggests that Regan's position, like Singer's, involves an endorsement of weak species egalitarianism and nothing stronger.

More controversially, Regan points out that the outcome should be the same even if the lives of a million dogs were at stake. While we might understand these given circumstances where only four lives in total could be saved (the scenario which Regan imagines), the worse-off principle does seem to suggest something else, i.e. that the saving of the lives of all four humans would be a better option even if we could save their lives only at the expense of the million canine lives. Saving three humans and all the dogs would violate the principle. The lives of the dogs would always have to be sacrificed if it could prevent a single human coming to greater harm. At this point, three suspicions emerge. Firstly, the position may not even be a weak form of species egalitarianism. Instead, it looks like a heavily qualified acceptance that humans matter more than non-humans. Secondly, if we can sacrifice animals for humans in extreme cases or *when the chips are down* then perhaps we should be entitled to experiment on them for the greater human good under regular circumstances, just as Singer's approach has always seemed to allow (a key claim made by Singer himself in the above-mentioned exchange). Finally, while there may be many differences of nuance and language between Singer and Regan, what they offer now looks very similar and so there is no basis for the idea that a rights approach, along Regan's lines, ought to be regarded as the default position for supporters of animal liberation.

The first concern, that any form of species egalitarianism now falls, can be at least partially answered by pointing out that Regan is concerned with *most cases*. If one of the humans in the lifeboat is cognitively impaired and would not be harmed so greatly by death (because fewer preferences would be frustrated), we may then have grounds for saving the dog rather than this particular human. The problem for Regan is that this will be the exception rather than the norm. And while he will not be favouring the humans because they are humans he will, nonetheless, usually be favouring them. Whether or not this approach—the endorsement of what I have called weak species egalitarianism—allows him, or Singer, to escape from a charge of speciesism will depend on how the latter concept is understood. If it involves tending to systematically favour humans in matters of life and death, and doing so for whatever reasons, then the position would appear to be speciesist. This is the suspicion of abolitionist critics such as Joan Dunayer and Gary Francione who hold that, in lifeboat cases, there simply is no principle to which we can systematically appeal: sometimes it will be right to save the humans and sometimes it will be right to sacrifice one of them for the sake of the dog plus others. And, for Dunayer especially, if the theory systematically favours the humans under normal conditions then the theory is inconsistent with any genuine, meaningful form of species egalitarianism. The only true form of species egalitarianism would then be what I have called strong species egalitarianism.

Regan fares perhaps rather better with regard to the second concern. What we may do in extreme, lifeboat situations, if we have not ourselves deliberately brought them about, is rather different from what we may do in circumstances of harm which we *have* deliberately contrived. Lifeboats are not laboratories. If I can sacrifice the life of one person to save two others when all three lives are threatened, it by no means follows that I am entitled to abduct that person from the streets and harvest their organs, or subject them to tests, just so long as I use their body to save the lives of the other two. The context matters. A similar consideration applies when we shift from humans to animals. If we deliberately bring about a laboratory experimentation situation then we are no longer innocent parties. If four experimenters deliberately strand themselves at sea with a dog, which they want to kill, in order to bring about its death with justification, the circumstances would *not* be normal and Regan would not automatically be required to countenance the dog's death to save the experimenters' lives.

Finally, there seems little doubt that Regan's qualifications of his harm principle, while plausible in their own right, do tend to blunt the radicalism of his position and thereby the extent to which he can reasonably claim to be presenting a more uncompromising defence of animals than Singer. However, we may have to consider their respective responses to a fuller range of empirical cases before suggesting that the theories are (more or less) normatively equivalent, i.e. equivalent as guides to action. As we have seen in the case of animal experimentation, where harm arises under circumstances which humans have deliberately brought about, Regan's position does seem to entail a guarantee of restriction that Singer's position may not. If the maximal outcome happened to be yielded by some invasive experimentation which is in the greater interest, while still considering all interests equally, Singer's utilitarianism may offer no way to block it. And it is considerations of this sort, together with a preference for the language of rights, which have led abolitionist critics of Singer and Regan to be more understanding of the apparent weaknesses of the latter than those of the former.

THE PROBLEM OF NEGATIVE RIGHTS

One final respect in which Regan's approach has deeply influenced subsequent, rival and critical, accounts of animal rights, is that his focus is on **negative rights**, i.e. rights not to be harmed, rights to be left alone, rather than **positive rights**, in the sense of entitlements to be supported and enabled in various ways. The rationale for this is that if someone is a rights-bearer of any sort then they will have a claim against others to deliver or protect this entitlement. In other words, some or all agents will have duties towards them. If these duties become too demanding then the account of rights may start to seem extremely impractical. It may seem like an account of ethics for some world other than our own. With regard to animal rights, the most obvious case where this matters is in relation to wild animals. It is one thing to say that animals, of whatever sort, have a right not to be killed for our culinary pleasure. But it is quite a different matter to say that they have a right to protection in the face of life-threatening dangers. The former merely requires us to stop slaughtering them for food. The latter might well require us also to protect them from predators. This would be an approach which could turn out to be ecologically unsustainable if adopted on any extensive scale. It would also involve favouring some creatures over others. If we police the wild, what do we do with the predators? How natural would their lives be under such a regulated system? Do we say that, ultimately, their lives are less important than those of their prey?

While Regan's approach is altogether too scholarly to have been adopted in detail as the guiding influence on animal advocacy, his restricted, negative-rights approach has nonetheless become the norm for a substantial section of the animal rights movement. This has been the case for some time now, even to the extent that a future is envisaged, by many animal rights activists, in which the only animals still in existence will be those who can be left to their own devices, those who do not need our regular support or intervention to survive. This would exclude descendants of many of today's domestic pets from existence as well as descendants from much of today's livestock. With regard to such creatures, the advocacy of a negative-rights approach has become coupled with the advocacy of **extinctionism** with regard to creatures whose dependency on humans is deeply entrenched. By controlling breeding, major lines of descent are to be brought to an end.

But while Regan's focus on negative rights avoids the problem of excessive demandingness, albeit at a price, it runs the risk of becoming *insufficiently* demanding. If we look at the case of domestic animals and take them rather than wild animals as our model, it may then seem obvious that we typically do have a great many positive responsibilities towards other creatures. And even with wild animals, in some cases we may build up expectations which we then have a duty to fulfil. If, for example, I feed birds every day at the start of winter, altering their pattern of movement and food-sourcing, it then seems plausible to say that I then have a responsibility to continue doing so until food sources again become plentiful in the spring. And what matters here is the *relationship* and the associated cultivation of *expectations*. All other things being equal, we should not lead animals to expect something when we are not going to deliver it. By virtue of my actions, the birds may well have a right, even a right in the fullest sense, to continued support. Considerations of this sort may lead us to accept that many animals with whom we regularly interact have entitlements which go far beyond simply being left alone.

A standard response to this move towards a more inclusive, positive-plus-negative conception of rights is to point out that the norm is for animals to be independent of humans and that a primary or exclusive focus on negative rights simply acknowledges this as a fact of nature. Put simply, it is wild animals who are truly natural. Domesticated creatures, by contrast, are a human contrivance, nature gone askew. Bringing about their non-violent extinction through a curtailment of breeding would then help to bring about a situation in which only the truly natural animals were alive and only negative rights were held by them. There are, however, at least two problems with such a view. Firstly, it requires us to buy into an anthropocentric mythology that domesticated animals are simply our creation. This is precisely the kind of mythology which relational accounts of animal ethics have criticized. We are not gods or the creators of animal beings. Rather, we may be closer to being what Donna Haraway refers to as co-evolutionary partners. We help to shape them and they help to shape us (albeit, their shaping of us is a little more subtle than our own brute-force approach). For Haraway, domestication has always been a case of co-evolution rather than a matter of denaturalizing human control. Secondly, even if the mythologies were correct and domesticated creatures were primarily or exclusively the product of human action, mere artefacts made by us, this would in no way render them second-rate or unnatural. Otherwise, almost all of nature would qualify as second-rate or unnatural. Human impact is everywhere. (And saying this is very different from suggesting that human control is just as extensive—impact and control are very different phenomena.) Added to which, even if domestication, in the first place, was originally wrong, this does not mean that we should now end it. As a parallel case, most existing nations have emerged through injustice and the violation of rights, through land-grabbing and cultural oppression at their borders. But this alone does not imply that we should now cease to recognize the nations in question. They may still be the best game in town.

CONCLUSION

What Regan presents is a subtle and nuanced account of animal rights but, overall, it is not clear that he manages to accomplish quite what he sets out to do. Once the detail is worked through, the position on offer does begin to look very close to Singer's in key respects. Their shared commitment to weak species egalitarianism is a case in point. And the liberal standards of equality which both extend to include animals can be challenged as either going too far or not going far enough. Yet there does remain a baseline commitment to delivering some kind of heavily qualified account of species equality. In some respect, humans are taken to be no more important than non-humans. For Regan as well as Singer, the argument from marginal cases plays a pivotal role in establishing this, albeit Regan's formulation seems to have some advantages over the hypothetical version presented by Singer and especially a closer proximity to our sense of what can and cannot be done.

FURTHER READING

Regan's key texts dealing with animals are *The Case for Animal Rights* (Berkeley: University of California Press, 2004 [1983]), *Animal Rights: Human Wrongs* (Lanham: Rowman & Littlefield, 2003) and *Defending Animal Rights* (Urbana and Chicago: University of Illinois Press, 2001). For a useful analytic breakdown of some key aspects of Regan's position see Mark Rowlands, *Animal Rights: Moral Theory and Practice* (Basingstoke: Palgrave Macmillan, 2009).

For alternative perspectives on the grounding of rights, see Joel Feinberg, 'The Rights of Animals and Future Generations', in his *Rights, Justice and the Bounds of Liberty* (Princeton: Princeton University Press, 1980), 159–84; and Alasdair Cochrane, *Animal Rights without Liberation* (New York: Columbia University Press, 2012).

For Mary Anne Warren's criticism of Regan, see her *Moral Status: Obligations to Persons and Other Living Things* (Oxford: Oxford University Press, 1997).

For the concept of the naturalistic fallacy (which appears on p. 247 of Regan's *The Case for Animal Rights*), see William Frankena's classic essay, 'The Naturalistic Fallacy', which is reprinted in Andrew Fisher and Simon Kirchin (eds), *Arguing About Metaethics* (London and New York: Routledge, 2006), 47–58. Frankena disputes the understanding of the concept which Regan takes more or less for granted.

4

CONTRACT THEORIES

Singer and Regan base their accounts of the moral standing of animals on the intrinsic properties of the animals in question, considered apart from any relations to others: many are sentient, feel pain, have preferences, and are (in Regan's terms) **subjects-of-a-life**. Of the two, Singer refuses to be drawn into any metaphysically deep exploration of, or talk about, inherent value or discussions of why moral judgements are made true by virtue of the properties in question. Regan, by contrast, is more forthcoming about metaphysically deep matters. He commits to the idea that there is a connection between being a subject-of-a-life (with all that entails in terms of sentience and an orderly experience of the world) and having equal **inherent value** with all other such subjects. And, while he too may avoid certain kinds of involved metaphysical speculation about the precise relationship between natural properties and inherent value, the correlation of the two suggests that animals not only have rights, but that they do so as a blunt fact of nature, no matter what social conventions are in place, and no matter how animals relate to humans and to each other. This makes Regan not just a rights theorist, but a **natural rights** theorist.

It also provides a source of persistent unease. There is a widespread suspicion that a complete inventory of nature would not include any such thing as rights. In the slightly uncharitable, but tellingly, critical words of Alasdair MacIntyre, we should not believe that there really are such rights for much the same reason that we do not believe there are witches or unicorns, i.e. our best attempts to discover such things have failed. (For MacIntyre, character traits are more obviously real and ethically significant.) Sensitivity to this charge, that natural rights are a kind of fiction, and a concern to avoid appealing to deep metaphysics, has also led many (perhaps most) contemporary rights theorists to be far less naturalistic in their account of rights, by either basing rights talk on something more tangible and clearly real—such as interests (with strong interests entailing duties on the part of others)—and/or by an appeal to rights as the product of certain kinds of rationally defensible social convention. These options make rights simultaneously less of a natural *given* and instead more relational.

Such approaches have the further advantage of marrying well with liberal political norms. Talk about inherent value in the case of animals is unlikely to secure agreement. It is a topic on which otherwise reasonable agents can and do disagree. This is a crucial consideration for those who incline towards liberal values. A commitment to liberalism is, after all, generally couched in terms of a refusal to impose conceptions of the Good on others, upon private individuals. What this means, in practice, is that if reasonable agents can disagree on some matter then they should not (ordinarily) be legally compelled to take a particular side, they should not be compelled to acknowledge the inherent value of non-humans through a system of legally specified rights. This will leave animal rights advocates in the awkward position of (a) having to abandon a cornerstone of political liberalism; or (b) having to accept that the moral rights of animals should not be legally enforceable; or (c) having to provide some other justification for legislative protection and for the legal recognition of animal rights. In which case, the inherent-value story does no useful political work (except, perhaps, that of reassuring the faithful, those already committed to animal rights). For **animal advocates** whose activities are heavily geared towards legislative changes, such as an ending of the property status of animals, only the final option is a serious contender.

Because of considerations of this sort (metaphysical doubts and the difficulty of securing agreement) the dominant view within rights theory is a more relational appeal to the idea of a contract rather than non-relational natural properties. If you and I enter into a contract, there will then be various reasonable expectations that we will have of one another. The compellingness of this simple consideration can, in turn, be underpinned in various ways but it is, at least, something which most of us, in our capacity as rational agents, can readily appreciate. As a basis for entitlements of various sorts, we might be inclined to say 'Who could ask for anything more?' Expectations which arise from agreements are the kinds of things that we might also (again reasonably) expect the state to take an interest in and sometimes to enforce. If, for example, I enter into a contract with you to set up a business, but then I abscond with our joint funds, I can hardly complain if I am then legally required, even compelled, to make amends. It is difficult to imagine a modern, complex society in which this might not be the case. In practice, just so long as a contract is fairly entered into and fairly framed, the social convention is that contracts do establish mutual obligations of an ethical and, sometimes, legally enforceable sort. (If contracts are not fairly entered into then matters are quite different and a contract may be struck down.)

The idea that fair and reasonable contracts do, in some sense, form the basis and justification for ethical and legal norms is a very old one. However, the importance which has, more recently, been assigned to the free market as a model for human relations has also helped to reaffirm the idea that key social institutions are based on something akin to fair and mutually beneficial agreements by self-interested parties. And here, the suggestion is not that there must be some actual formal agreement, enacted by agents or inherited from their predecessors, perhaps in the form of an agreed ancient constitution. The suggestion of contract theory is, rather, that the *equivalent of* a contract exists either because tacit, unspoken consent is given to some arrangement, or else because reasonable agents *would* explicitly agree to it if placed in the right situation to deliberate about matters. A situation of the latter sort is usually referred to as the **original position** where rules are debated and settled. The background thought is that, although for some arrangements (such as business contracts) explicit consent is required, for a large class of cases it is reasonable for me to act *as if* we already had a formal agreement in place. If, for example, you and I go for a drive to some remote place in your car and, on arrival, you collapse, I should act as if there was an agreement about my using your car in such situations to get you to a hospital, or at least to get you to a place where there is phone coverage. I should do this even if I realize that the car is your pride and joy and that ordinarily I would not be allowed anywhere near the driver's seat. I can presume that, nonetheless, under emergency circumstances, you would agree to my action if only you could do so. A worry here is, of course, that I might overestimate what you would agree to as a result of misunderstanding, bad deliberation or self-interest.

One obvious difficulty with extending this approach to animals is that, while many animals may be agents, shaping events through their actions and choices, they do not seem to be the kind of agents who could ever, under any circumstances, engage in deliberation about social policy, legal entitlements or political affairs. They could not, under any real circumstances, give assent to a contractual arrangement even if it was a contractual arrangement which granted them rights. What they would, hypothetically, agree to in any imagined original position cannot then shape our obligations towards them because, even in an original position, they would not be able to agree to anything. Put simply, animals could not be parties to a contract. This consideration has led the most important figure in modern contract theory, John Rawls, to suggest that our obligations towards each other, as rational human agents, are covered by contractual relations, but our obligations towards animals are not. While sometimes it is assumed that this places animals beyond ethical consideration, it does not necessarily do so. Rather, for Rawls, they are covered by other, non-contractual considerations. Animals, then, are not to be neglected, they are certainly not to be subject to cruelty (that would clash with liberal norms) but they are nonetheless outside of the contract by which we humans are bound to one another. This ensures, from the outset, that their moral standing cannot be equal to ours.

Others have disagreed. Some have even suggested that the animal-excluding understanding of contracts which Rawls set out in *A Theory of Justice* (1971) is far more flexible than Rawls himself allowed. Even so, there are two very different ways of considering animals as having ethical standing by virtue of contractual con-siderations. The first, as indicated, draws on Rawls and yields a basis for animal rights claims which is very different from Tom Regan's appeal to inherent value. But there is a second and quite different way of appealing to the contract idea, one which suggests that, in a sense, animals can be parties to a contract, but it is a contract which yields a defence of practices such as slaughter and meat-eating. Over the past decade, this alternative way of including animals within some sort of contract has become the dominant way of defending ethically informed meat-eating. In the US it is associated with the best-selling food writer Michael Pollan and in the UK it has been advocated by the celebrity chef and eco-advocate Hugh Fearnley-Whittingstall. These two quite different, Rawlsian and non-Rawlsian, ways of appealing to a contract are considered below.

APPLYING RAWLS TO ANIMALS

Rawls invites us to imagine an original position in which rational agents have to deliberate about which rules they are to live by but they do not happen to know what natural gifts or talents they have or where they will be situated in society as a result of any agreement. They deliberate rationally but behind a **veil of ignorance** where peculiarities and idiosyncrasies are removed. If inequality in the distribution of material goods is sanctioned by their deliberations, then the individual deliberators might find themselves at the top of society when the veil is removed. But they might equally well find themselves at the bottom. This absence of foreknowledge is geared to exclude certain kinds of prejudice and unfairness.

Rawls believed that uncertainty about where agents themselves would be placed would lead to caution. Agents would try to ensure that, however badly they were situated, the harms to which they would be exposed should be minimized. (This is the **maximin principle**.) Deliberation would result in an agreement which protected the position of those who were least well off. Tolerable inequalities of wealth would then be linked to this goal, with inequalities accepted if and only if they improved conditions for those at the bottom of society. This is, by any account, an extremely loaded picture, one which appeals to far more than our bare, shared rationality. It involves, and is driven by, an independent commitment to distributive justice. Rawls agrees: accounts of an original position will always be loaded. In a sense, what rules the original position yields will always depend on how it is set up. And so we need some non-arbitrary guidelines for carrying out this task. For

Rawls, this would involve going with the best available practice which we have for deliberation. This best available practice will involve the use of intuitions (e.g. those concerning fairness and justice) in order to shape our theories, and the use of theories to qualify and evaluate the defensibility of our intuitions. The overall aim then is to secure a **reflective equilibrium** between intuitions and theory. This is a plausible description of actual, well-ordered ethical deliberation. And so, while Rawls does appeal to a special kind of thought experiment (his account of deliberation in an original position behind the veil of ignorance) there is less of a problem concerning remoteness from familiar ways of deliberating ('moral Esperanto') than there is with Singer and Regan. However, the very procedure of reflective equilibrium which brings him close to a familiar kind of ethical reasoning plays a suspiciously large role. Critics have suggested that it is reflective equilibrium, rather than the idea of any sort of contractual arrangement, which is doing all of the important work. Talk about what agents would agree to behind a veil of ignorance might then seem to contribute very little in its own right.

Even so, by appeal to the basic intuition that animals could not contribute to a contractual discussion, Rawls excludes them from his specification of an appropriately constituted original position. This has seemed, to Regan, a decisive reason for basing animal rights on inherent value rather than on a contractual agreement. Others, such as Mark Rowlands, have argued that this is too hasty. He suggests that Rawls is *not clearly* excluding animals at all, but is acknowledging that it *looks like* they might be excluded. Whatever we make of this reading of the text, it seems that we can very well use a broadly Rawlsian, or modified Rawlsian, approach to make contractualist sense of the entitlements of animals. Suppose, for example, that you were to decide on a set of rules for the relations between humans and animals, but that you did not know whether you would turn out to be human or animal. Would this not shape your deliberations so that you would be strongly inclined to minimize the harm that you might suffer if, after the decision was made, you turned out to be a bird or a pig? Rowlands uses this example to suggest that the Rawlsian veil-of-ignorance approach *can* and *ought* to be applied.

Interestingly, this kind of thought experiment, involving ignorance about future standing, is not a new idea. It looks remarkably similar to one of the best-known ancient justifications for vegetarianism, given by followers of Pythagoras (c.570–490 BCE): if the souls of humans might find their way into the bodies of animals in the next life then the creatures which we eat might be lost friends, relatives or even parents. We too might then end up being eaten in turn by those we love and care for. If we regard this primarily as an ethical point (rather than as a metaphysical claim about future lives) it may be used as a way to bring us closer to an appreciation of the predicament of non-humans in a human-dominated world. If, given a chance to live again, we did not know whether we would be the human consumer or the consumed pig, we might then think twice about the merits of bacon. And, in line with Rawls, a key consideration then would be to minimize the harm that might befall us. To do this, out of an enlightened self-interest, we might well require more than the liberal restriction of cruelty. We might, from such self-interest, reject even the most humane forms of slaughter. Deliberation which is close to the Rawlsian approach thus seems to have a very long pedigree. It involves a way of thinking about matters which is not a local or modern aberration.

CRITICISMS OF A RAWLSIAN APPROACH

In the case just considered, appeal is made to an application of the Rawlsian maximin principle, i.e. the rule that we should seek to maximize the position of the least well off. This would, as noted above, be agreed to by reasonable, self-interested agent in the original position, just in case the least well off turned out to be themselves. This principle has not, however, seemed like an obvious claim to everyone. After all, some of us are gamblers, prepared to risk great misfortune in return for the opportunity to thrive. And some of us only care about our further existence if it includes those goods (such as special rational capabilities) which we associate with being human. If, for example, you knew that you were going to be turned into a pig then perhaps you would simply not care about survival, or about how you might be treated, once the transformation has taken place. Perhaps all that you would worry about would be pain. And it is not in any way obvious that indifference towards, or even outright hostility to, further survival under such conditions should be taken as the mark of any lack of rationality. Indifference to survival as a pig seems, instead, to be a matter on which reasonable agents might disagree.

It will then become difficult to guide deliberation towards any actual agreement if (in the light of this kind of consideration) we do not all buy into the maximin principle. The danger is that rational agents, discussing matters behind a veil of ignorance, would simply fail to agree on what should be done in the case of animals because self-interested future protection might not shape and steer their deliberation. And if rational agents might disagree then, insofar as we remain true to a broadly liberal position, legislative restriction is (again) probably inappropriate. This might lead us to wonder whether an appeal to Rawlsian-style contractarianism could ever *actually* deliver a plausible account of animal rights which was truly capable of rivalling Regan's more naturalistic approach.

We might also have broader concerns about the very idea of the veil of ignorance and about the applicability of such an approach to the standing of animals. Two concerns in particular stand out. Firstly, one of the most important general critics of Rawlsian theory, Michael Sandel, has suggested that when Rawls invites us to bracket out pretty much everything that is distinctive about ourselves, with the exception of our bare rationality, he seems to be suggesting that what we *are* essentially, what is at the very core of our being, is nothing more than pure rationality itself. While Kant might have approved of this sort of claim, others have regarded it as palpably false and have suggested that the self is much 'thicker': we are beings with history, constituted in particular circumstances and constituted, in part, by our complex and particular relations to others. The whole idea of the veil of ignorance presupposes a misleadingly thin 'unencumbered' self.

Supporters of Rawls have been quick to respond that this is not so. To imagine the stripping away of various properties from the rich beings that we so manifestly are, is simply to deploy an imaginative device which can help us to deliberate with a little less bias than usual. For example, it removes the potentially distorting influence of any appeal to properties for which we have no responsibility and for which we may be able to claim no credit. But it does not presuppose anything deeper about the nature of humans or about the nature of the self. Yet it is not obvious that this reply will make a revised version of Sandel's problem go away. If we really are thick and complex beings, it is not obvious that we really *can* imagine ourselves as stripped-back deliberators. Such an act of the imagination might turn out to be impossible, a cover for deliberation in which various influences continue but become concealed. They may seem to be sent into exile but they continually return in all manner of subtle and covert ways. Or, perhaps, we might succeed in stripping away some crucial aspects of our concrete selfhood and thereby imagine a very different sort of self. In which case, what authority would such an odd sort of creature have over how beings like us should actually live? If we are not in fact imagining the truest part of who we are, when we think about deliberation behind the veil of ignorance, then why should such deliberation be regarded as authoritative for beings like us? It may begin to look suspiciously like an appeal is being made to some utterly external authority quite unlike any actually existing rational ethical agent (a prospect of outside authority which Kant would have found abhorrent).

Secondly, it seems obvious, and it seemed clear to Rawls, that actual deliberators, even in a hypothetical original position behind a veil of ignorance, simply could not *be* ignorant of what species they belonged to, while they remained capable of actual deliberation. If we deliberate at all, we must be the kinds of beings who can do so and this more or less guarantees that we must be humans (or clever aliens ... and we do not know of the existence of any of the latter). It seems then that, at best, deliberation behind a veil of ignorance can be *about* animals but it cannot *involve* animals and it also cannot *involve* agents who are in any way unsure about whether or not they might turn out to be animals. To be at all uncertain about the latter, a deliberator would have to take a special religious commitment behind the veil of ignorance, i.e. a genuine belief in reincarnation under altered physiological conditions. And it is precisely this kind of metaphysical commitment that talk about the veil of ignorance is supposed to leave behind.

If we accept this point, we may still retain duties towards animals for some reason, especially duties concerning the avoidance of cruelty, but as Rawls does seem to affirm, this would *not* be the result of our being bound to them as we are to contracting parties. This, in turn, may lead us to the important and plausible idea that the beneficiaries of a contract need not themselves be contracting parties. There are, after all, humans such as infants and the mentally impaired, who also could not be deliberators but whose interests would have to be taken into account by deliberators, otherwise an appeal to the veil of ignorance will fall flat because it will take us too far from our intuitions about what is right and wrong. But now, as with Singer and Regan, an appeal to marginal cases seems to be doing a good deal of work. For marginal humans, advocacy rather than their participation in the drafting of a contract is required, and much the same might also be said in the case of animals. But if this is so then an unwelcome difficulty arises. On traditional social contract theories, enlightened self-interest is presupposed to be the driving force of the whole process, making it extremely unlikely that *anyone* other than a contracting party, or those they have a direct concern for, could be a beneficiary *for their own sake*. We might then appeal to the possibility that the interests of contracting agents and the interests of others must be bound together in some way. But that appears rather hopeful or fortuitous. It might apply in some cases but it is difficult to see why we should expect this always to be the case. And if it is not always so then the recognition of animal standing by contracting agents would be a hit-and-miss affair, sometimes but not always.

Furthermore, once a system of advocacy is included to cover the interests of non-deliberators, the whole approach does begin to look far less contractual, far less a matter of what we owe to each other by virtue of what we might agree to if we were each to look at matters rationally and dispassionately. A symptom of this is that at least one prominent attempt to extend Rawlsian considerations to cover animals (the account by Rowlands, already mentioned above) altogether dispenses with the idea that any manner of dialogue must be imagined to occur behind the veil of ignorance. Instead, we need only appeal to a single rational deliberator from whom various traits and foreknowledge have been stripped. And this, again, may lead us to question whether the appeal to the veil of ignorance is doing any of the heavy lifting. Again, it may seem that the real work is being done by intuition or perhaps by Rawlsian reflective equilibrium: the shaping of a theory by appeal to intuitions and the evaluation of these intuitions by appeal to the resulting theory.

It may also be worth noting that, in recent years, rival versions of the original position, which have yet to be applied systematically to animals, have also dispensed with deliberation behind the veil of ignorance and have focused more simply on the idea of reasonable agreement or what we might justify directly to one another. Such an approach draws especially on work of Thomas Scanlon and dispenses with much of the disputed Rawlsian machinery. In doing so it endorses the core liberal claim that when all reasonable agents can disagree, their scope for action should not normally be constrained. While this approach might allow more easily for the inclusion of deliberation *about* animal well-being (but not deliberation *as* or *with* agents who might turn out to be animals), it looks likely that it might not be sufficiently constraining to satisfy animal advocates. Cruelty would, no doubt, be ruled out (just as it was by Rawls and by liberals more generally) but slaughter, meat consumption, and experimentation might still be permissible.

DOMESTICATION AS A CONTRACT

As indicated previously, as well as being used in a more or less Rawlsian manner to make sense of animal rights, contract theory has also been applied as a way of justifying ethically informed meat-eating. The argument that meat-eating is part of a deal, one which is in the interest of the animals themselves, has primarily been deployed in the broader public arena, in the press, in best-selling non-fiction and on television rather than in academic texts. Disseminated widely, it has become the dominant ethically informed justification for meat-eating. So, for example, when, in 2012, the *New York Times* ran a competition for essays in defence of the practice, the most frequently recurring argument among the finalists was one or other version of the contract argument: *we give them something and we take something in return*. Because of the arena in which it has been shaped, some generous reconstruction is required to render the argument more precise and more open to evaluation.

Let us suppose that a domesticated animal, a randomly selected pig with no unusual attributes, is killed at what we shall call the time of death and let us call some earlier time, when it was deliberately brought into existence precisely in order to be killed, the time of birth. Unless it is already suffering in some dire way, we can hardly say that it benefits, at the time of death, from being killed. Let us, to make matters even clearer, suppose that it is not euthanized but instead is slaughtered for meat production. While it looks rather obvious that the animal cannot possibly benefit from being slaughtered at the time of death, its interests at other points in time may be slightly less clear. Harm at the time of death might conceivably be worth trading off against benefits at other points in time or *overall* across an entire life. Candidate benefits could be (1) the advantages of being fed and cared for prior to slaughter and/or (2) the advantages of existing rather than not existing. The animal's *being there* rather than not *being there* might be said to depend, in some way, on a process of breeding in which an event of slaughter is anticipated.

Of these two candidate benefits, only the second looks as if it could count as a fair and just exchange. It might be claimed that food and care are enough to warrant a trade-off but it is tempting to say that they are simply not equivalent to a life and so they cannot be *fairly* exchanged for the latter. (Nobody could be entitled to slaughter a lodger, no matter how much bed and board they had received beforehand.) However, the second set of advantages cannot so readily be dismissed. An opportunity of life, traded in return for an ending of life, does look like an exchange of equivalents and therefore, all other things being equal, it appears to be not just a fair exchange but an exemplary instance of fair exchange. We may call this the **opportunity of life argument**. Variants of the argument have been advanced by defenders of best meat-eating practice, people such as Michael Pollan and Hugh Fearnley-Whittingstall, and by welfare-concerned defenders of wider patterns of meat production and consumption such as Temple Grandin. While the latter draws on the basic intuition that it is better to live than not to do so, the former draw on a slightly more nuanced popular account of the evolutionary position of domesticated animals by Stephen Budiansky, *The Covenant of the Wild* (1992). The argument does, however, have some further precedents. Most notoriously, there is a nineteenth-century Darwinian monograph by Leslie Stephen, 'Ethics and the Struggle for Existence' (1896). Stephen argued that if there were no bacon there would be no pigs. Similarly, if the whole world were Jewish, there would be no pigs. (There is a veiled element of anti-Semitism in his brand of Darwinism, something which needs to be detached from the defence of meat, for the sake of plausibility.) And so the true friend of the animal, or of domesticated species, is the agent who is not overcome by religious dogma or by sentimental squeamishness and, instead, accepts the evolutionary facts of the matter by participating in the food cycle, a food cycle which provides the rationale for individual creatures to be given an opportunity for life. We get our meat, the individual animals get to live and the species to which they belong gets to survive. It is a fair deal all round.

Now let us suppose that, during his life, however short, existing definitely was in the interests of our randomly selected pig, that he was not reared under intolerable conditions. And let us allow that, were it not for the fact that he was going to be slaughtered at some point in time, he simply would not have existed. Let us also allow that, in the absence of the cultivation of animals in sterile jars, the responsibility for bringing a pig into existence cannot actually be discretely located but is somewhat spread around. But let us nonetheless accept that, *in some qualified sense*, this particular pig really was brought into existence by a human or by a group of humans in order to be slaughtered for meat. What this seems to point to, a little paradoxically, is the way in which the existence of a system of slaughter is not just advantageous to humans but advantageous to animals also, to animals such as the pig. On the basis of this, it may be argued that Leslie Stephen was right, that the curtailment of meat production and consumption would conflict with animal interests.

If it works, this argument could provide a way to avoid basing the justification for meat-eating on the overriding importance of human preferences or on our relatively trivial culinary pleasures. It might also, conceivably, sidestep the issue of whether or not animals may legitimately be said to have rights such as a right not to be eaten or only to be eaten under certain restricted circumstances. After all, rights (or at least *some* rights) may be the kind of thing that can be waived in the interests of their bearers, or the kind of thing that may be waived on their behalf by some suitably concerned advocate. Presumably, if any such right existed and could be waived, animals would agree to its being waived when this served their best interests. This seems to allow the whole territory of rights talk to be avoided, and by avoiding it, the argument seems to provide an elegant and streamlined defence of slaughter that does not rest on any dubious background assumptions about radically limited animal competences or about their second-rate moral standing. Like the Rawlsian approach, it also does not seem to rest on any unsettling and deep metaphysical assumptions about inherent value or its absence. On the face of matters, the argument appeals solely to the interests of animals themselves and it does so in a particularly effective manner. While some animal advocates (**abolitionists** in particular) insist on advocating **extinctionism** for domesticated creatures, through a curtailment of breeding, conscientious meat-eaters welcome the opportunity for all manner of domesticated creatures to live worthwhile and contented lives. This is not a comparison which favours abolitionist advocates of animal rights.

Moreover, the argument (on any plausible formulation) is tied only and exclusively to conscientious meat-eating, if not necessarily to best-practice meat-eating (whatever that might turn out to be). It cannot be used to justify industrial forms of livestock farming and slaughter which offer the opportunity of a life that is not worth living. It can only be used to justify those forms of farming and slaughter which offer a life that is, on the whole, worthwhile. Even so, we may wonder about precisely *when* animals, such as our imagined pig, are supposed to benefit from the system of slaughter and precisely *which* actions they are supposed to benefit from. At the very least, it is implausible to claim that they benefit from the actual act of being slaughtered. At the very least, we may require that talk about their benefiting from slaughter must be shorthand for the claim that animals benefit from other actions, the ones required to bring them into existence *for* slaughter. These are actions which will always have occurred prior to the animal's existence. In the case of our random pig, they will have occurred at, or prior to, the time of birth. However, any appeal to the benefits secured from such actions may seem vulnerable to an objection raised by the Victorian animal rights pioneer, Henry Salt: animals cannot benefit from events prior to their lives because benefits always require that the beneficiary enjoys the terra firma of existence. However, it should be noted that Peter Singer has, for some years now—and with a good deal of plausibility—suggested that this response does not work and that opponents of meat-eating ought to abandon it.

Rejecting the Henry Salt move need not require the embracing of a metaphysically odd assumption that interests can exist before their bearers. What it requires is that we separate the times of harms and benefits from the time at which a harmful action is carried out. Following Singer (and contra Salt) we may point out that creatures may be harmed during their lives by prior events. They may, be harmed by *in vitro* experimentation when the latter results in their gross deformity. Similarly, in the case of humans, if someone plants a bomb in the marketplace today but it doesn't go off for another three generations, the time of harm and the time of the harmful action will be quite different. The perpetrator of the action in question also cannot defend it by saying that none of those ultimately harmed were alive when the action was carried out, none of them enjoyed the terra firma of existence. But if creatures (human and non-human) can be harmed by events which have taken place prior to their existence, it will no longer be obvious that they cannot benefit from events which have also taken place at some similarly prior point in time. There is no obvious reason to assume that there is any asymmetry between harms and benefits (at least in this context, other circumstances may be rather different). First come the actions and later come their benefits. Separating out the two need not be regarded as metaphysically worrying. And so the appealing simplicity of the opportunity of life argument is preserved.

Returning to the example of the random pig, what seems to be the case is that the animal slaughtered at the time of death really has benefited, during his or her life, from some actions carried out at or prior to the time of birth, actions which were tied to the prospect of slaughter and which did form part of a system of *breeding for* slaughter. But, awkwardly for advocates of this argument, the pig's existence after the time of birth can only be said to have depended on the continuation of a system of slaughter insofar as the latter provided the rationale for feeding and care. Once alive, the pig could have continued to exist in the face of the complete collapse of meat production. At least some pigs do survive quite well when they escape from farms and slaughterhouses and go feral in woodland. Contingent circumstances might even have worked in favour of the pig enjoying a good life as a result of such a collapse. And so, what the pig benefits from, by existing, is not actually an ongoing system of slaughter but rather a historic one.

However, this does not necessarily imply that there are no benefits to any animals from the continuation of slaughter once some group of animals already exists. It might still be maintained that after the birth of the random pig, the continuation of a system of slaughter would eventually be beneficial for those animals who did not yet exist at the random pig's time of birth and who, instead, came into existence at some later point in time, having also been bred for an ongoing process of slaughter. Each animal bred for slaughter, which enjoys a worthwhile life, benefits during its lifetime from the existence of a system of slaughter *prior to* its life. And so, as a way to provide a justification for the continuation of slaughter at the time when the pig is finally killed, someone might appeal to the interests of animals other than those about to die, although this may be regarded as slightly problematic because it is more of an appeal to interests that will exist in the future rather than the current interests of actual animals. While we might not want to discount such interests (however construed) because of the knock-on effects that such discounting would have when we come to deliberate about our responsibilities to future generations of humans, it is not at all obvious that such interests will automatically trump the significant interest that already existing beings will have.

Alternatively, a rather different sort of appeal may be made. And this, perhaps, is where the opportunity of life argument ends up when it seeks consistency. An appeal may be made not to the interests of individual creatures (whether existing now or in the future) but rather to the species as a whole. This is Stephen Budiansky's position and it is strongly supported by Michael Pollan. The benefit to animals is not an individual benefit but a species benefit. Supporters of Singer and Regan, whose inclinations are strongly individualist, may tend to automatically discount this approach on the grounds that it is only individual creatures who have interests at all. Species cannot have preferences. They cannot experience pleasure. Nor can they suffer. As interests are to be understood in such terms, species simply cannot have interests. And this may be more in tune with broadly liberal, individualist, sensibilities rather than any Darwinian-influenced collectivism. But even if we accept some revised version of the latter, and accept that it does make sense to talk about species having interests, and doing so in their own right, we may still wonder whether the survival of a species under conditions of breeding for slaughter (with all of the gerrymandering of biological structure that this involves) is actually worthwhile. Sometimes the price of survival may be too high. Intuitions here may differ about how repugnant the future of a species (such as our own) would have to be before it was no longer worthwhile. This does, however, take us some distance away from the charmingly simple argument that without bacon there would be no pig. It takes us to precisely the place where the opportunity of life argument does not want to go, i.e. into the metaphysical depths where reasonable disagreement may be expected.

CONCLUSION

Death is such an extreme form of payment that any requirement that it be paid, in return for benefits received, might have to rest on an explicit prior agreement by the payee. An implicit contractual arrangement might not be good enough. And even if the payee, the ultimately slaughtered creature, did benefit from such an agreement, there are some advantageous contracts which may be too problematic to be accepted as valid. We would, for example, always strike down any deal involving slaughter, or even partial dismemberment, as utterly monstrous in the case of humans, even if the interests of the latter could be shown to be promoted by such an arrangement. Bringing into existence may well confer a benefit to humans for which gratitude is genuinely due. Perhaps it would be wrong to uphold the position of the disaffected teenager who says 'I didn't ask to be born.' But we ordinarily restrict any duty of gratitude and any resulting notion of obligation. Not all societies have done so, but patriarchal systems in which the head of the family has the power of life and death are part of a world well lost. And while defenders of capital punishment sometimes do hold that a human life *is* something which can be owed (and that it is intelligible and right to view matters in this way) it would be morally idiosyncratic to say that a human life could ever be owed in the absence of having taken another life or caused it to be taken by some third party. We would not, accordingly, be tempted to revert to some rather antiquated norm.

There may even be a sense in which it is part of our understanding of what it is to be human that we see such deals as indefensible in spite of free choice, parity of exchange, and any further benefits that the deal might involve. Even if all parties agreed, did so explicitly and kept on agreeing to the terms of the deal, we would still view it as a void contract and strike it down in the human case. It is part of a *prior* evaluation of animals, an expression of the fact that we already see them as *lesser*, that we do not regard them in the same way. The upshot is that once a contract is set out in clear terms, it no longer appeals *simply* to animal interests but rather it requires a large background assumption about *legitimate ways of seeing* non-human creatures. The appearance of being able to sidestep the familiar arguments about the relative standing of the human and the non-human may thus begin to look deceptive. More narrowly, if a conception of animal rights is accepted as legitimate and is held in conjunction with an endorsement of the opportunity of life argument, the rights in question will then have to be of a sort which differ radically from the life-protecting rights which are in play in the human case. And so the charm and simplicity of a direct, assumption-free appeal to animal interests is lost. So too is any obvious reason why an animal advocate should accept the presupposed assumptions as the legitimate background to human/animal contractual arrangements or to deliberation about animals more generally.

FURTHER READING

The exclusion of animals from any social contract is set out in John Rawls, *A Theory of Justice* (Cambridge, MA: Harvard University Press, 1999 [1971]). For an attempt to extend a Rawlsian framework to animals, see Mark Rowlands, *Animal Rights: Moral Theory and Practice* (Basingstoke: Palgrave Macmillan, 2009). Against Rawls, Mark Coeckelbergh makes a case for the inclusion of animals within the sphere of justice in his paper 'Distributive Justice and Co-operation in a World of Humans and Non-humans', *Res Publica* 15(1) (2009): 67–84. Similarly, Robert Garner includes animals within the sphere of justice in *A Theory of Justice for Animals* (Oxford: Oxford University Press, 2013).

For the opportunity of life argument see Stephen Budiansky, *The Covenant of the Wild* (London: Phoenix, 1997 [1992]); Hugh Fearnley-Whittingstall, *The River Cottage Meat Book* (London: Hodder & Stoughton, 2004); Temple Grandin, *Animals Make Us Human* (New York: Houghton-Mifflin Harcourt, 2009); Tony Milligan, *Beyond Animal Rights* (London and New York: Continuum, 2010); Michael Pollan, *The Omnivore's Dilemma* (New York: Penguin, 2006); Henry Salt, 'The Logic of the Larder', in Tom Regan and Peter Singer (eds), *Animal Rights and Human Obligations* (Englewood Cliffs, NJ: Prentice-Hall, 1976); Peter Singer, *Practical Ethics* (New York: Cambridge University Press, 2011 [1980, 1993]); and Leslie Stephen, 'Ethics and the Struggle for Existence', in *Social Rights and Duties*, vol. 1 (London: Swan Sonnenschein & Co., 1896). For scepticism about rights theory, see Alasdair MacIntyre, *After Virtue* (London: Duckworth, 2007).

5

WHAT IS SO SPECIAL
ABOUT HUMANS?

At the heart of the Singer and Regan positions there is a shared challenge to the special standing of humans. Yet this standing is not easily disposed of. In both accounts, a sense of the specialness of humans seems to be covertly reaffirmed. (At least, this is how more radical critics such as Gary Francione have read matters.) Most of the time, on their accounts, when it comes to a choice between human interests and animal interests, it is the former which will win out, albeit because they will generally be greater interests. And this may seem rather too convenient: humans are not to be given priority because they are humans, but nonetheless they are still to be given priority. This may be species egalitarianism of a sort, because any *direct* appeal to species membership is ruled out, but it champions a weak sort of equality when compared with a more full-blooded **strong species egalitarianism**, the rejection of human privilege in all forms, indirect as well as direct. Yet once the specialness of being human has been challenged we may find ourselves at a loss to explain exactly what it is about *us* that makes us so special. In the light of the arguments set out by Singer and Regan, and especially the **argument from marginal cases**, the answer may not be at all obvious.

HUMANS AND PERSONS

Although humans *are*, as a point of fact, assigned a very privileged standing in a great deal of ethical discussion, we are often privileged in the guise of persons, and these two concepts are not quite the same. Personhood (as it has come to be understood in the philosophical literature) requires self-awareness over time, rationality, agency and moral autonomy. Only **moral agents** are persons, **moral patients** (beings who cannot exercise rational choice in moral contexts) are not. The upshot is that a person need not be a human but they must be able to deliberate in a more or systematic manner about themselves and about how to act *in* the world or *as part of* the world. And while we might imagine various sorts of non-humans who could fit this description, the genre which does so most regularly is a branch of fiction (science fiction). In the world with which we are familiar, typical, unimpaired and adult humans are the only non-controversial examples of personhood that we have. Attempts to claim that other sorts of familiar terrestrial animals might also qualify, or that some animals are, in Peter Singer's terminology, 'near persons', are usually treated with some caution. They may seem either to overestimate the rational capabilities of the creatures in question or else they may seem to place the bar for personhood too low precisely in order to allow non-humans to qualify (a move which is made by Gary Francione).

Primates, or more precisely the great apes, such as chimpanzees, gorillas and bonobos, are a special exception. These are the most human-like of creatures. They are our closest living biological relations. Unless we define personhood in terms of verbal communication (which seems somewhat arbitrary as well as likely to result in unwanted human exclusions) or in terms of linguistic complexity (which might be more plausible) it is going to be difficult to deny that the great apes exhibit significant components of personhood or personhood in a rudimentary, prototypical form. In their case, a terminology of 'personhood' or at least that of 'near persons' has won considerable support. This may also, at a stretch, apply in the case of cetaceans: aquatic creatures such as whales and dolphins whose lives render them mysterious. Even so, livestock clearly do not qualify and neither do pets. Nor do the vast majority of creatures who are routinely subjected to the experimental system. With the personhood of these animals denied, and with the attribution of personhood more or less limited to humans (or to humans plus human-like animals), the claim that persons are the *most* valuable beings that we know of seems to confirm the strong intuition which most of us have about the special importance of humans. It seems to confirm that we really are as important as we have always assumed and the fact of our personhood may turn out to explain why this is the case.

The trouble is, as the argument from marginal cases indicates, not all humans happen to be persons in the relevant demanding sense. In fact, none of us are persons for the entirety of our creaturely lives. As infants, we did not have the relevant kind of fully developed rational agency, nor will we enjoy such agency should we reach the later and more extreme stages of dementia. Similar considerations apply to humans in a coma or in a permanent vegetative state. Biologically, all such beings are still humans, but none will count as persons (again, on the standard and demanding account of the latter). And while this might license us to prioritize the interests of those humans who *are* persons over those who are not, we might still worry about devaluing such humans by classifying them as non-persons. We might also worry about how close this puts these individuals to being 'subhumans', which is an idea with a dreadful history, one associated with colonial conquest, the systematic murder of indigenous peoples and ultimately with the Holocaust.

As matters stand, we would not think it at all justified to treat those humans who lack personhood, or full personhood, in the way that we currently treat many animals. We would not think it reasonable to kill them for even the most serious of reasons unless perhaps our reason was that their lives had, in some irreversible way, become unbearable to live. We would certainly not think it right to own them, keep them as pets, or subject them to slaughter in order to bring about some or other sensual pleasure through their exquisite taste, the excitement of hunting them with hounds, the feel of their flesh on our bodies. But if they are not persons, then just why any of this is wrong in their case, but legitimate in the case of animals, may be something of a mystery. Here, as a response, it will do no good to call on familiar claims about potential, a claim which is drawn directly from debates about abortion. One of the established argumentative moves within discussions of the latter involves accepting that while fetuses are clearly not *actual* persons they are nonetheless *potential* persons. As such, they are entitled to the full standing of personhood or to some large portion of the latter. Perhaps in a trade-off we would always favour an actual person over a potential person, or we would favour an infant who is closer to personhood over a fetus. But this is consistent with accepting that potential persons still have some, many or all of the key entitlements which go with personhood, i.e. a certain kind of robust moral consideration, protection and recognition of interests which can only be trumped by the interests of other humans.

Whatever we make of such a potential-person move in the abortion case, it does not seem to carry over well into our deliberations about why infants and extreme dementia sufferers matter in the way that, for most of us, they indisputably do matter. Setting aside imaginative but unrealistic scenarios in which dementia sufferers recover, those in the later stages of dementia, when so much is gone and (perhaps mercifully) little is left, are in an irreversible condition with no potential to become persons ever again. But here we might argue that respect of a more or less full sort is still due to them because they once *were* persons. Yet, while this looks like a plausible get-out clause, it will clearly not apply when we look at the other end of human life. Some human infants who suffer from debilitating neurological conditions have not been and never will be in a position to develop a full rational personhood. They are not, never have been and never will be persons in the classic sense outlined above. Unless we shift the boundaries of personhood (in ways which will invite in all sorts of non-humans) they do not have either personhood or potential personhood. Indeed, it seems partly definitional of who they are that they will never become persons in the classic Kantian sense of autonomous rational agents. There are always some humans for whom a potentiality claim cannot realistically be made.

Perhaps, we might think that such humans are not exactly potential persons but rather that they are something else, an approximation of another kind. While they may not have all that it takes to be a person, and will never have all that it takes, they have at least some of it and rather more of it than any familiar non-human. They may, for example, have some degree of self-awareness, something close to a complex appreciation of time, and some rudimentary rational capabilities. Singer's terminology of 'near persons' may be appropriate for use. But the trouble with such a view is, again, on this matter the argument from marginal cases does seem to be right. Whatever traits or capabilities we happen to focus on, there will always turn out to be non-human animals who have these very same traits or capabilities, and they may do so to a greater extent than some humans. And here, when thinking of such well-equipped animals, we might think not only about the special case of great apes but also about the case of unimpaired adult cats, dogs and pigs, all of whom have a more sophisticated awareness of self and surroundings than a newborn human infant. They need such awareness because they are part of a world in which they cannot afford to be as dependent and vulnerable as a newborn human infant. Evolution has equipped them with more than the latter need in order to survive.

Accordingly, because these non-human animals are nearer than some humans to being persons, we would have to give their lives priority over the humans in question if we were genuinely being consistent, fair and basing our judgements of value on the properties which creatures (humans and non-humans) actually possess. On the hypothetical version of the argument from marginal cases, if we think that it is wrong (indeed very wrong) to kill such human infants or late-stage dementia sufferers, then we ought not to kill any animals with equivalent properties or more developed capabilities. On the categorical version, *because* it is wrong (indeed very wrong) to kill the former, we ought not to kill the latter or, indeed, to harm them in various ways. All other things being equal, we ought also to give such non-humans priority or parity when it comes to accessing medical equipment and life-saving resources.

Against this, many of us still have the strong intuition that marginal-case arguments go badly wrong, that they miss something basic. It is tempting to say that, without any appeal to personhood or to special properties, humans are simply and ultimately more important *because they are human*. Michael Pollan advances just this position in *The Omnivore's Dilemma* (2006), a best-selling exploration of contemporary dietary options and their ecological and social cost. He describes his own brief and failed experiment with vegetarianism breaking down in a restaurant while he read Singer with growing frustration, repeatedly scribbling 'because they're human' in the margins. On first glance, this does look suspiciously like a form of species prejudice but perhaps the problem here is conceptual. Perhaps a difficulty arises—an exclusion of something important—when we try to get the concept of person (which is associated with a special series of properties) to perform work that the concept of human is simply better at doing. Admittedly, ethicists may have good reasons for buying so heavily into the idea that we should, on many occasions, prioritize the concept of person. But is the concept of a person really our best conceptual tool in familiar morally troubling contexts such as abortion or in discussions about life and death for beings like ourselves?

The abortion issue may be indicative because it provides a context in which ethicists have repeatedly noticed that prioritizing the concept of persons can invite us to say all sorts of strange and implausible things. Suppose, for example, that I hold abortion to be permissible, not nice, not pleasant, not something that one could be *pro* in the sense that one can be pro-liberty, but nonetheless permissible, a legitimate choice that a woman might make. And suppose that I defend abortion rights because pregnant women are persons but a fetus is not. (Our conception of personhood would have to be extremely minimal to think otherwise.) This hardly licenses me to try and console a woman who has had a miscarriage by pointing out that what she has lost was not really, or not yet, a person. It is tempting to say that, if I should attempt this kind of consolation with a woman in such a situation, and even more so with a woman whose child has been stillborn or whose infant has died in its cot, this could only be because I am in the grip of a peculiar sort of theory or because I am suffering from some manner of mental health problem. Nor is the fact that this consideration simply would not console based on a sentimental parental delusion, an overestimation of exactly what has been lost. The problem is not that pregnant women imagine more than there is to the life that they carry, or that the parents of newborn infants imagine more than there really is to see. Rather, the problem is that their connection to this living being does not seem to be captured at all well by appeal to personhood or even by appeal to potential personhood. And so we may begin to think that there is something very wrong with the discussion when cast primarily in these terms.

Instead of trying to get the concept of personhood to do all or most of the work, it may make more sense to think of abortion as the ending of the early stages of a *human* life, and to think of newborn infants as *humans* irrespective of their potential or level of mental development. In spite of appeals to potential persons, this is the driving thought for at least some opponents of abortion. Similarly with dementia sufferers, no matter how extreme the victim's condition, is it not important from a moral point of view to assert that the sufferer may lose their personal identity or their selfhood, that they may lose whatever intrigues philosophers at any given time, but they can *never* lose their humanity? Surely, there is still always something there which calls for our respect? But what this something is cannot properly be explained by appeal to any special set of properties such as the complex awareness of time, awareness of an apparent persistence of being, deliberative powers of an abstract sort, and so on. It seems tempting to say that, in some *difficult-to-explain way*, the fact that there is always something worthy of respect, and perhaps even love, is a morally significant fact about dementia sufferers, no matter how extreme their condition becomes. The fact that *we*, who engage in moral philosophy and ethics, share a common humanity with *them* seems to be a morally significant fact about us both or, rather, about all of us collectively. This is a consideration which Raimond Gaita, in particular, has appealed to in order to challenge the more individualist approaches of Singer and Regan.

THE APPEAL TO A BOND

What this points to is the idea that the argument from marginal cases, or at least formulations which in any way resemble the versions set out by Singer and Regan, completely miss the point. Appeals to the special importance of humans may not be grounded in any view about special properties. Rather, the special importance of humans may be bond-based. That is to say, it may best be understood in relational terms. We can, of course, retain the language of properties, if we are absolutely determined to do so, but the properties that matter will be relational properties rather than properties of the sort that Singer and Regan have in mind, properties which we can make sense of without reference to other beings. And the most obvious candidate for such a relational property is that of shared membership of the same species.

This does, of course, invite the response that appeal to the species bond is yet another instance of **speciesism** in the sense of *a prejudice in favour of our own*. Mary Midgley has, however, suggested otherwise. She has suggested that the similarities between this kind of favouring and sexism, anti-Semitism or racism are superficial. It is an important feature of the former prejudices that they are all social constructs. They are the products of history and have emerged more or less in the order given, with racism making a surprisingly late appearance. To state an obvious but important point, we don't have anti-Semitism before we have Judaism. Sexism is a little more complicated, but our best anthropology and most plausible accounts of history give it a history as well. And this fact, that each of these prejudices has a history, may give us hope for their comprehensive eradication. They are, perhaps, things which can be overcome although none of them is near to being ended.

According to Midgley, a special attachment to our own species is rather different. It is a basic, biologically given fact about being human. *Every* human society has regarded humans as having special standing, even those in which human life has been, relatively, cheap. This makes it such a deep fact about who we are that the prospect of ending this attitude towards humans is effectively the prospect of ceasing to be human. Coupled with the familiar idea that *ought* implies *can*, it is simply mistaken to say that we ought to cease privileging the human for the obvious reason that we cannot do so. The fact that we privilege humans is part of the background conditions for morality rather than a stance which can be amended within it. It is important to note, here, that Midgley's sympathies are, nonetheless, very much *with* animals, at least in the sense that she is a strong advocate of animal welfare. She is very far from offering some apology or excuse for a continuation of the status quo. Yet what she does offer has been questioned. It relies on the idea that ethics is strongly bounded by biology and more specifically by species identification.

Moreover, she thinks rather more highly of the latter than Darwin did. For Darwin, group identification tended to be geographically localized. On such an alternative account, it is simply not true to say that animals generally favour their own kind. Territorial animals will, for example, tolerate various other sorts of creatures in their midst, but not members of the same species. And, contrary to Midgley, Darwin believed that this extended to humans also. We are not discontinuous with other types of creatures. The species bond, identification with other humans as set apart from other creatures in a special way, may be an extension or modification of more primitive, or at least more basic, biologically hard-wired localized group identification, but it is not itself built directly into our inherited traits or (in more contemporary terms) it is not hard-wired into our genes. A more strictly Darwinian position may suggest that any species bond will be neither simply a natural given nor ineradicable. And such a view is supported also by those who have less sympathy than Darwin with the project of tracing our constitutive features back to sheer biology. Within the humanities, one of the prevailing ideas of the past several decades is that many (or all) of the key aspects of our identity are, in some sense or at some level, socially constructed.

Yet, even if true, this need not automatically rule out the possibility of a bond-based defence of the special importance of humans. On the latter, Midgley may still be right. After all, when someone appeals to our common humanity, must they be suggesting that all humans matter in a special way because we are part of the same privileged species? There are versions of the idea that all humans matter, versions such as Gaita's which do not seem be about a biological bond but rather about more of a social, historically constructed bond. As an alternative way of understanding such appeals Gaita has suggested that the sense of 'human' that is in play in many of our appeals to a shared humanity is *not* the same as the biological concept of *Homo sapiens*. Instead, he points to contexts in which, like 'person', '*Homo sapiens*' also fails to do the right sort of work. When, for example, a Shakespearean character says of doomed soldiers that they are 'mortal men' he is saying far more than he could by pointing out that they are '*Homo sapiens*'. Similarly, when the wronged Shylock points out that he too, and other Jews like him, can bleed, laugh and desire revenge, he is not ultimately appealing to the capacities which go with our species membership. Rather, he is appealing to aspects of what it is to be human, i.e. what it is like to lead our kind of life. Similarly, when I suggest that Tolstoy shows a deeper understanding of humanity in *War and Peace* than the script editors of soap operas seem to show, I am not suggesting that the latter would be unable to identify the *Homo sapiens* from a line-up of dogs, cats and humans.

In the relevant contexts, when we talk about our shared humanity and about *being human*, we do not seem to be using biological or species concepts at all, although this is an area where confusion can easily arise. Imagine, for example, that the all-too-human Captain Kirk says to the alien Spock, 'you are the most human of us all' and Spock, wrinkling his brows, says 'I find that ... insulting.' In such an exchange, the two would be at cross-purposes. They would be talking about very different things. To speak of our shared humanity in the way that Kirk (or Gaita) does, is to appeal to a concept of shared circumstance, shared vulnerability and mutual obligation which has been built up precisely as a way to combat important forms of prejudice such as racism and anti-Semitism. Indeed, we do not need to look to Gaita in order to encounter this kind of discourse about a common humanity. It is persistently present in the writings of Gandhi and, more recently, the Dalai Lama (both of whose sympathies have been very much on the side of animal advocacy and very much against animal slaughter). Confronted with such appeals, it may do no good to call into play the argument from marginal cases in order to say (quite correctly) that not all biological humans share our vulnerability, circumstances and kind of life. It will do no good because what is appealed to is a form of community membership and this is what the individualism of Singer and Regan seems least able to cope with, i.e. the context of moral communities within which we live and have our being. And the norm with regard to communities is to accept that while there are multiple ways of becoming a community member, one of the most important ways of doing so is being born into it: roughly, if your parents, or if the right parent, is a community member, then you are a member also irrespective of your competences, talents or special properties.

THE DANGERS OF A COVERT SPECIESISM

A shift in focus away from the biological idea of species and towards that of a socially constructed human bond suggests that contract theories—in spite of their problems and weaknesses—have been looking in the right direction: not to accounts of the inherent value which we have as isolated individuals, but to our social being, to some idea of social relatedness or connection. Where they go wrong may then seem to be in their preference for the rather strained metaphor of a contract which pictures fairly conducted commerce as the ideal ethical relation (a view which critics of capitalism may, with some justification, find objectionable). But when appeal is made to a social connection or to a bond among humans, we may wonder about just what kind of bond is in question and how talk about such a bond can avoid collapsing back into the simpler idea of shared species membership. There may be a concern that bond talk, or community talk, must function merely as a respectable way of smuggling a prejudicial species loyalty back into the picture.

Indeed, among those who stress the idea of humanity as a common bond there are a range of positions, from those who regard it as strongly independent of species talk (such as the Wittgensteinians Cora Diamond and Raimond Gaita) through to those who regard it as a bond which is ultimately species-based (such as the influential political philosopher Elizabeth Anderson, as well as Mary Midgley). It certainly could not be regarded as a bond which is entirely independent of species membership and, in practice, once we set aside the imaginary circumstances of science fiction, it is shared *only* by members of the species *Homo sapiens*. This does not seem to be an accident. It yields a sense of the importance of precisely the creatures which we are inclined to favour. At the very least, this keeps significant speciesist dangers in play. We may, after all, be misled into treating our shared bond of humanity as if it involved the shared possession of greater inherent value than any other kind of creature. And it is difficult to see how that could avoid being a prejudice.

To understand this danger, let us consider the circumstances of a familiar, indeed familial, bond. If you have a sister, she may favour your interests over the interests of others in some (not all) contexts. She may regularly buy you presents at predictable points in the year when she does not buy presents for strangers, and she may do so even though the money spent on these presents could conceivably do far more good if handed over to a charity. In spite of such considerations, we ordinarily allow that the bond which joins siblings together *can* justify a reasonable partiality. Such a reasonable partiality is not ordinarily regarded as favouritism or prejudice. (We might even take steps to make explicit some universal entitlement to treat siblings in this way so that the same rules apply to all.) But this does not mean that your sister is then licensed to assume that, in the larger order of things, you have more inherent value than anyone else: strangers, acquaintances, adversaries and so on. In this respect, it is difficult to see how talk about a special human bond could differ. It may license special treatment of those with whom we share the bond, but this does not tell us anything at all about the comparative importance or value of those with whom the bond is not shared. An affirmation of our common humanity does not entail that *we* have more inherent value than *them*, although it is tempting to imagine otherwise.

But let us suppose that the idea of our common humanity is set out in minimal terms without any claims about humans mattering more than non-humans. On such a minimal account we might say that a shared humanity is a legitimate source of reasons for acting; that it is a social rather than straightforwardly biological or species bond; and that it warrants preferential treatment under some circumstances. Set out in such terms, would a commitment to the importance of our shared humanity still involve any commitment to speciesism? Would it be right to regard it as a speciesist discourse? A tempting answer might appeal to the idea that a discourse commits to speciesism *if and only if* it involves or *is* coupled with some claim of greater human value (a **greater value thesis**) or, more radically, with a claim that *only* humans have worth (a **sole value thesis**). But talk about the ethical significance of humanity as a bond does not entail this and it is not obvious that it needs any such dangerous supplement. Difficult though it may be for us to accept, even if we affirm the ethical importance of a shared humanity it may still be the case that some or all non-human animals *are* just as important as some or all humans. Singer and Regan, and with them the argument from marginal cases, may then be correct about this crucial point.

Even so, this kind of affirmation of a special human bond may still give too much ground—it may still be construed as prejudice if we adopt the rather more inclusive understanding of species prejudice set out by Joan Dunayer in *Speciesism* (2004). On this approach, a viewpoint does not even need to appeal directly to species membership in order to be speciesist. Rather, it is speciesist if it tends in practice to systematically favour humans over non-humans for whatever given reason. And here we may suspect that a commitment to the importance of our shared humanity might operate in just this way even when qualified by reassurances that it is by no means an affirmation that humans matter more in the grand scheme of things, or have more inherent value. It will be consistent with **weak species egalitarianism**, but the latter will itself count as an endorsement of speciesism (which is just the way in which Dunayer and other **abolitionists** see matters—weak species egalitarianism is not egalitarianism at all).

However, granting the special ethical importance of a human bond (a special importance for us) need not always operate in a way which does actually favour humans. Indeed, an appeal to our common humanity might be used in quite the opposite manner, as a response to historical injustice, as a way of acknowledging what *we* have done to *them*. For example, suppose we accept that animals have suffered terribly through experimentation and that humans have both inflicted and benefited from such experimentation. This could well act as a reason to prioritize animal interests when faced with some conflict or dilemma. The fact that *we* are advantaged humans and *they* are part of the disadvantaged (even wronged) group, and that *they* have been harmed by humans like us, could be grounds for forgoing the advantages offered by any further animal experimentation (should there be any such advantages). Whether or not a commitment to a shared humanity tends to operate to the advantage or disadvantage of animals, and whether or not it will lead us, in practice, to prioritize human interests over animal interests, will depend on the way in which we make sense of such a shared humanity and the obligations that it carries. In practice, it may perhaps tend to be 'something in-between', operating in a way which is simultaneously or successively helpful *and* dangerous. It might then be difficult to regard it as speciesism of a disguised or subtle sort.

Considerations of this sort may also lead us towards caution about appeals to our humanity, it may involve taking on too great a burden, too much of the burden of our history. (And this might, perhaps, be just what shapes a certain kind of puritanical position, a sense of our human guilt.) But such caution can be pressed too far. Risk is, as Jacques Derrida has often reminded us, the precondition for certain kinds of accomplishment—ethical and other sorts of accomplishment. If we are then convinced that appeals to a shared humanity do have their place, it may perhaps be tempting to make sense of them in fairly minimal terms which cannot be misused to uphold serious animal harms. Yet, what happens once we pare back the requirements for a commitment to our shared humanity—in order to avoid any suggestion of speciesist prejudice—is that it may begin to look like an imagined, rather than genuine, community. The sense of connection to others may be too weak or contrived to fit an ethically approved pattern. (And real communities do not seem to be like this. Community identity is always a mixed and varied phenomenon.)

To bolster a sense of the genuineness, the authenticity of the human bond, we can draw on a series of analogies with membership of the same ethnic group or nationality, socio-historic groupings which do seem to involve bonds of a substantial or robust sort. And here again we do tend to think that such bonds can legitimately be action-guiding. For example, the attitude of the descendants of slave-owners towards some matters should not be quite the same as that of the descendants of slaves. (They may be required to bear certain things in mind.) Similarly, the children and grandchildren of Holocaust perpetrators should, perhaps, have a certain sense of ethical obligation that the children and grandchildren of Holocaust survivors need not have. Both may have ethical responsibilities which are connected to a remembrance of the past, but they are not exactly *the same* responsibilities.

Awkwardly, the analogy between a shared humanity and such bonds, or the bond of family membership appealed to earlier, may seem fairly weak. After all, we generally *know* our family members. By contrast, we do not and cannot know all humans. So, how could we possibly have any analogously strong bond with them? But perhaps, in relation to personally knowing other members of the group, a better analogy might be drawn with the members of a nation or of a religious community, and especially a persecuted religious community. In the latter case, we might think of what is involved in being Jewish. There is a certain sense in which responses to prejudice directed against the group not only involve a sense of connection with *unknown* others now living but also a connection to *unknown* others down through the ages. And these are individuals with whom any personal intimate connection is not only absent but, in principle, impossible. Shared membership of a community does not seem to require or presuppose intimacy. Non-intimate ties are the community norm. And this favours the claim that our shared humanity can involve a genuine, robust relation to others.

There are also two important reasons why anyone who is suspicious about appeals to a shared humanity ought to be cautious about challenging the analogy between humanity and recognized communities. On the one hand, many or all communities whose standing as communities is accepted are themselves partly constituted by fictions and by a slightly mythologized understanding of shared bonds. Nations seem to be very much like this, even to the extent that reasonable individuals can disagree about whether or not they are part of the same nation. Not all Scottish people see themselves as British. Some do, many do not. However, as a cautionary note, there is also something slightly unsatisfactory about this argumentative move. Explicit appeals to nationality are made all the time while explicit appeals to our common humanity are much rarer. The mythologies of nationhood are such an everyday practical matter that a tolerant pragmatism requires us to accept the genuineness of the communities in question. Talk about a common humanity may seem instead to belong to utopian and aspirational political discourse, and to grey areas of international law, rather than belonging to a pragmatic realpolitik.

On the other hand, if this argumentative move fails because talk about a common humanity is aspirational, a second move becomes strengthened. Raimond Gaita argues that the human bond is not only robust but is also so deep that nothing like it could ever be shared with other creatures. Mary Midgley believes that, on the contrary, a mixed community of humans and non-humans is already a genuine fact. Others still, such as Cora Diamond, regard it as closer to a realistic possibility. Those who, in the interests of animal advocacy, wish to defend the possibility of a real mixed community may have to make sure that they do not raise the bar for the genuineness of shared community membership too high for such a community to be possible. This will impact on the ways in which the idea of a shared humanity may safely be challenged. If the bar is kept low enough to allow a mixed community to be a possibility, it may then be difficult to deny that a real human community is already a fact. Yet it is the kind of fact which may warrant *occasional* partiality albeit without doing anything at all to justify familiar and ongoing animal harms such as slaughter or experimentation. I may, after all, be entitled to favour a fellow countryman or family member or a member of the same ethnic group under some special circumstances (if we find ourselves thrown together as strangers in a strange land) but this does not mean that I can send anyone else to the slaughterhouse.

CONCLUSION

There are, of course, many concepts which we are better off without: 'nigger', 'Yid', 'bastard', 'half-caste', 'bitch', and so on. These are concepts for which we ought now to have no use, except perhaps where their use genuinely subverts their traditional role, concepts which we may hesitate even to *mention* let alone *use*, because mentioning itself can be a special form of use. But when such obviously offensive exceptions are set aside, there is a case for being cautious about attempts to render ethically laden concepts redundant. The whole approach of Diamond and Gaita towards talk about humanity is premised on the broader attitude towards the tasks of philosophy, tasks which include safeguarding ethics against the danger of a loss of concepts. If we fail to show caution in this regard, we may then lose something which we need in order to make adequate sense of our world.

There is, however, a discourse which seeks to enrich our conceptual repertoire precisely by challenging our socially constructed idea of a stable, fixed, humanity. Indeed, seen in a certain light, the idea of humanity and of a special bond with our fellow humans may seem to be rather old-fashioned. Over the past two decades 'posthumanist', 'transhumanist' and 'accelerationist' discourses have emerged, differently nuanced and contrastingly labelled discourses which look towards a near future in which our descendants may be very different sorts of creatures, and to a present in which we are already, in a sense, more or other than strictly human by virtue of the technology with which we engage—and which may now seem to be, already, a part of us. Anyone who finds their iPad or Kindle a vital piece of daily equipment may be ready to acknowledge that we are, in various senses, already akin to the mixed beings that Donna Haraway has (rather dramatically) called 'cyborgs', and that we are simply shy about acknowledging the change that has occurred. Perhaps we should embrace this change as a matter of *going beyond* the human towards something better, or at least towards something more enabled. Any residual attachment to the ideology of humanism, or to a sense of a shared humanity, may then seem to be terribly backward-looking. In line with one strand of such posthumanist thinking, Cary Wolf has suggested that the very idea of the human (and not just the idea of a human community) is a kind of mythology. And what is in play here is not the mere biological concept of a member of our species—it is the very idea of the human, the socially constructed idea of *what is left* when we exclude all the animals, from horses to snails and from dogs to seagulls.

The most systematic, but also subtly qualified, extension of this point comes from outside of the posthumanist discourse, from Derrida's *The Animal That Therefore I Am* (2006). But unlike stridently posthumanist discourses, it has no agenda of disposing of the concept of the human, rather than problematizing it. In fact, Derrida's discussion is characteristically involved and elusive but the key points are clear: (1) talk about the human is always implicitly talk about the non-human; (2) the division of human and animal is more of a contrast (a distinction which applies only in certain ways and only up to a point) than a rigid dichotomy; (3) the contrast of the human and the animal is a limited one, precisely because the conception of the human depends on the conception of the animal, which in turn is used to refer to all sorts of creatures taken to be united precisely because of their lack of humanity; (4) the danger that talk about the animal introduces is one of missing the particularity of the individual creature (the creature before whom we are capable of embarrassment when we feel ourselves under its gaze); (5) the concept of the human, even to the extent that it is appropriate, is relational through and through.

The latter point has been further explored by Haraway in *When Species Meet* (2008) and in *The Companion Species Manifesto* (2003). Like Derrida, for Haraway, the lowest unit of analysis is always the relation, a connection to the other. We tend to think of ourselves, in the liberal tradition of Kant and Mill, as autonomous, stable and separate, thoroughly apart from the creatures, pets or companion animals we may own or at least care for. However, companionship by its nature takes two. If such animals are our companions, we are also their companions. And what this entails is that even if Singer and Regan are wrong and it is legitimate to acknowledge or endorse the ethical importance of talk about our humanity, the latter is still not to be regarded as a community which can be understood in isolation from other creatures and other communities. Any defensible sense of a common humanity may have to be constrained by insights of this sort, by an appreciation of the unspoken but relational aspects of being human, by recognition that there are others with

whom we are fellow creatures as well as others with whom we are
fellow humans.

FURTHER READING

For treatment of animals as persons, see Gary Francione, *Animals as Persons* (New York: Columbia University Press, 2008).

For bond-based accounts of the special standing of humans for other humans, see Mary Midgley, *Animals and Why They Matter* (Athens: University of Georgia Press, 1983) and Raimond Gaita, *Our Common Humanity* (Abingdon, Oxon: Routledge, 2008), *The Philosopher's Dog* (London: Routledge, 2003), and his more demanding *Good and Evil: An Absolute Conception* (London: Routledge, 2003).

For the limits of the human/animal distinction, see Jacques Derrida's *The Animal That Therefore I Am* (New York: Fordham University Press, 2008) together with Donna Haraway, *The Companion Species Manifesto* (Chicago: Prickly Paradigm Press, 2003) and *When Species Meet* (Minneapolis: University of Minnesota Press, 2008).

For the apparent obtuseness of the argument from marginal cases, see Elizabeth Anderson, 'Animal Rights and the Values of Nonhuman Life', in Cass Sustein and Martha Nussbaum (eds), *Animal Rights* (Oxford: Oxford University Press, 2004), 277–97; and Cora Diamond, 'Eating Meat and Eating People', in *The Realistic Spirit* (Cambridge, MA: MIT Press, 1991), 319–33.

6

THE HOLOCAUST ANALOGY

Appeals to the ethical importance of our common humanity rely on a strong, and perhaps also comforting, sense of the differences between humans and non-humans, even though these differences may be qualified in various ways. Those who support such appeals face a charge of clinging onto a sense of shared identification which belongs in the past and which draws, openly or covertly, on a special kind of prejudice in favour of our species. Even appeals to our humanity as a matter of a shared social bond, rather than a shared species membership, face the charge of repackaging prejudice rather than avoiding it. Those who insist on the ethical irrelevance of our humanity face a different problem, a danger of proving too much. They may be in a position to oppose harm to humans and non-humans alike, but they may find it hard to explain why iconic instances of extreme harm to humans are in any way special or worse than the everyday, ongoing processes of animal slaughter and experimentation. What occurs daily—in slaughterhouses which are within an easy twenty-minute-drive from where most of us live—may then seem to be not just appalling or wrong, but comparable to the events at Auschwitz or Dachau. They may find it difficult to reject a disturbing, even offensive, analogy.

AN OFFENSIVE ANALOGY

The analogy between animal slaughter and the Holocaust has become a familiar feature of the discourse on harm. Two equally familiar responses attempt to place it beyond the bounds of reasonable discussion. Firstly, some commentators such as Raimond Gaita have argued that the unacceptability of the analogy is not so much a matter of the attempted extermination of a particular group of people but rather is linked to the fact that it was humans who were killed, in the sense of murdered. For Gaita, this simply *must* mark a significant difference from the process of animal slaughter which may be wrong but does not seem at all like murder. This rests, however, on a prior acceptance of the distinctiveness of humans and cannot count as any independent evidence for the latter.

Secondly, and rather differently from Gaita, it has been maintained that the Holocaust itself is not just murder on an inconceivable scale. Rather, it escapes analysis or comprehension—any attempt to make sense of it must fail. We simply cannot grasp the enormity of the horror and so analogies with the Holocaust will always miss their target. But, while there may be an element of truth here, a refusal to try to make at least some sense of the Holocaust, and of its similarities to other instances of extreme harm, may be just as much a failure, albeit a failure of a different sort. This may be a subject matter on which our best deliberations do always fall short, but where deliberation is nonetheless not just permissible but an ethical requirement. What seems wrong would be allowing the Holocaust to drop out of view, to be forgotten. And, over time, there may now be a very real chance of this happening.

Yet, while analysis and comparison may be legitimate, even required, attempts to draw any close comparison with industrialized animal slaughter have tended to be dismissed as just too culturally insensitive to count as a plausible and legitimate argumentative move. The suggestion is not necessarily that animal slaughter can be defended, but rather that the case against it needs to be posed in a different way. And this sense of what is needed is about the bounds of acceptable discussion. Here, we may also allow that productive discussions are always bounded, they always have their limits. We may test and push at these limits, and they may shift over time, but they are always there. Holocaust denial, for example, is beyond the bounds of reasonable discourse because it relies on an utter determination to ignore the evidence (and there is a vast amount of it) which conflicts with the viewpoint of its supporters. There are also reasonable concerns about the sincerity of Holocaust deniers and about the likelihood that denial will simply function as a guise for anti-Semitism. Deployment of the **Holocaust analogy** is very different from Holocaust denial in all sorts of respects. It is evidence-based rather than evidence-discounting. It draws on the alarming facts concerning real similarities of process and on various sorts of causal connection between two kinds of killing. The architects of Auschwitz did not, after all, start from scratch. They were extremely efficient at what they did because they began from established systems of mass killing and from theories of rapid industrial production (Taylorism and Fordism in particular) which also shaped the stockyards of Chicago. Nor must an appeal to the analogy in any way deny the dreadfulness of the Holocaust although, for a critic who is utterly committed to the lesser standing of animals, it might seem to devalue the victims of the Holocaust by obscuring the unique awfulness of what was done to them.

As a cautionary matter, for the sake of the victims, survivors and their offspring we might consider it safest to adopt the latter standpoint. However, a difficulty here is that some of the most interesting uses of the analogy have come from Holocaust survivors and from individuals, embedded within the Jewish community, who in no way desire to devalue the terribleness of the events known to the latter as 'the Shoah', the catastrophe. Indeed, their whole point depends on a sense of its utter, uncapturable dreadfulness. It was, after all, the vegetarian Isaac Bashevis Singer who persistently pressed the analogy in a series of stories, written over the course of decades— stories such as 'The Letter Writer' (1964)— and who has advanced the notorious claim that 'for the animals, it is an eternal Treblinka'. Occurrences can also be found, in relatively recent times, in the pages of the left-of-centre Israel newspaper *Ha'aretz* (which has its critics). Various Jewish animal rights activists, and supporters of organizations such as PETA (People for the Ethical Treatment of Animals), have also affirmed that they do see uncomfortable connections between the mass murder of the Holocaust and industrialized systems of animal slaughter. The deeply felt need to save and to cherish animals, experienced by individuals with a strong and direct

Holocaust connection, is also well documented, and this too may shape matters. None of these considerations indicate a consensus on how the Holocaust is best spoken of and what connections to other instances of harm can be made. We might, however, feel that some analogies of the most disturbing sort can be used, but only by agents who have the right kind of connection to events, and this might make us uneasy about deployment of the analogy by anyone outside of the Jewish community or by anyone outside one of the other communities (such as Roma) which were targeted for extermination.

It may be read as a symptom of unease about the authority required to talk about these matters that very few **animal advocates** have been keen to wholeheartedly and consistently embrace the analogy. Fewer still have thought it a good idea to play up the analogy for publicity purposes. Although PETA did run a 'Holocaust on Your Plate' poster campaign in 2004, the campaign ran in the US but was banned in Germany. Yet, if what we adhere to is some manner of species egalitarianism, it is not immediately obvious why the analogy must be in any way misleading. While it may be impolitic and offensive to make a connection to the Holocaust, people are sometimes offended by that which is true. There are, after all, truths, and especially truths about ourselves, from which we would all like to hide. But the alleged truth about ourselves, in this case, would not simply be embarrassing. It would be utterly dreadful: we would be complicit in the moral equivalent of the greatest evil imaginable. If the analogy is a good one, we may then be no better than those who permitted and even tacitly endorsed the Holocaust. Bashevis Singer's own corollary to the predicament of animals is a harsh judgement on us: 'In relation to them, all people are Nazis.' This itself is a very doubled-edged comment. It appeals to our shared culpability, albeit it does so by using a terminology of 'people' rather than 'humans'. And this is symptomatic of the fact that Bashevis Singer, and many of those who support the insightfulness of the analogy, are not advocating the ethical irrelevance of the idea of humanity. Rather, they are appealing to our sense of humanity, and pointing to a shared wrong in which we *as humans* are complicit.

This too is an alarming idea, one which strikes at virtually all of us, meat-eaters, vegetarians and vegans alike. If there really is anything which is remotely akin to the ethical equivalent of the Holocaust going on everyday, and nearby, within our reach, it is hard to imagine that any of us do enough to oppose it. If this really is happening then we should perhaps be engaging in more than occasional leafleting and placard bearing, we should instead be physically liberating the animals and perhaps blowing up the slaughterhouses, just as our predecessors ought to have blown up the crematoria at Auschwitz, and the railway tracks which fed the concentration camps. It is in this sense that there is a danger of an argument for species egalitarianism proving too much. The latter may call on this striking analogy with the Holocaust, but the analogy may then sanction, even require, forms of activism far in excess of anything which is contemplated by any of the main animal rights groupings, including groups such as the Animal Liberation Front who do engage in covert activities.

SIGNIFICANT DISANALOGIES

There are, however, some striking disanalogies which animal advocates have pointed to in order to show that they are not required to press the analogy with the Holocaust too far, to the extent that it yields practical measures more appropriate to circumstances of war. Yes, there are obvious connections between the two systems of killing, such that the extermination camps *were* partly modelled on the Union Stock Yards in Chicago, but technical similarities do not necessarily entail ethical equivalence. The victims of the camps and of the extermination programmes were not killed for food as livestock are killed—they were murdered out of hatred and in the belief that they were closer to vermin than to livestock. They were also killed by those who, in every important sense, ought to have known better, those who may have been born into centuries of anti-Semitism but who were not born into centuries of mass killing. Their default position should *not* have been compliance.

This is not to say that there are no significant similarities between the mindset of Holocaust perpetrators and the mindset of humans who now work in slaughterhouses. It is tempting to say that both have engaged in practices which have a systematically dehumanizing impact (something which greatly and notoriously worried the Nazi hierarchy—considerable effort was taken to relieve the obvious psychological stress on perpetrators). But here, again, we may find it difficult to address matters realistically—we may figuratively or literally be lost for words, unless we allow that there genuinely is some shared sense of humanity which is partly constituted by norms governing the treatment of others, a sense of humanity which can be compromised or even betrayed by our actions. However, reactions to those who carry out such harms have tended to be very different. Holocaust perpetrators rarely engage our sympathies. The harm that they have done to themselves is overshadowed or silenced by a sense of the harm which they have caused to others. Responses by animal advocates to perpetrators have tended to be more mixed. Those who work in the experimental system are heavily stigmatized but the plight of low-paid workers in slaughterhouses has often been regarded rather more sympathetically, along the lines of: 'nobody should have to do such work'.

Even so, considerations of this sort, which address the mindset, motivation and even the social standing of perpetrators, may well establish at least some ethical distinction between these two kinds of killing. But we might regard it as a rather tenuous distinction in the light of the fact that, for the victims, the end result (death on a massive scale) is much the same. What would strengthen the ethical distinction is the finding of a difference which might be drawn in terms of the impact of actions and events on victims. Indeed, by prioritizing the attitudes and goals of the perpetrators we might seem to be already engaging in a moral wrong, an additional way of devaluing victims. The approaches of Regan and Singer may be useful in this regard. Because they subscribe to a **weak species egalitarianism**, they are both well placed to offer accounts of the ways in which the harms to victims differ. While Singer endorses the equal consideration of interests irrespective of where they are located (in humans or non-humans), he accepts that animals do not characteristically have the same interest in the continuation of life that an unimpaired, adult human has, because death does not frustrate their preferences (desires) in the same way. What this implies is that the harm to animals which arises as a result of slaughter is *not* the same as the harm to a human victim of technically similar (even identical) processes. With some fine-tuning with regard to the case of infants murdered in the camps, this creates scope to draw a major distinction between animal slaughter and the Holocaust in terms of the impact on victims rather than by appeal to the mindset of perpetrators.

The main problem that Singer's framework faces is the danger that a sufficiently large number of animal harms might well add up to the equivalent of a greater harm to a far smaller number of humans. Given that the vast number of animals killed annually runs into the billions, in terms of the overall harm, animal slaughter might again turn out to be just as bad, from a strict consequentialist point of view. And so, while Singer's framework allows a real ethical distinction to be drawn, it still faces a problem which stems from its utilitarian dimension. Any harm, no matter how extreme, might seem to equal a vast number of lesser harms. But surely, a vast amount of suffering from hay fever, no matter how inconceivably vast, could *never* equal the suffering of the Holocaust. It is difficult to imagine how we might even engage in any serious ethical discussion with someone who thought otherwise or who felt that this needed to be said. This danger of an aggregation of lesser harms is something against which any utilitarian approach will need safeguards.

Singer's own preference has been to avoid direct use of the analogy with the Holocaust while defending the legal and discursive entitlement of others to use it as a matter of free speech. When, in the 1990s, his supportive attitude towards euthanasia drew comparisons with the Nazi policy towards 'defectives', Singer pointed out that he had lost relations—all but one of his grandparents—in the Holocaust. The time lag in disclosure of this is, again, indicative of caution about anything which smacks of the attempt to make political capital out of a catastrophe. But while Singer has generally avoided the analogy, if we regard entitlement to deploy it as something dependent on the agent having the right kind of personal connection, then he does seem to have the kind of connection which could license its use. His reticence may then be symptomatic, but we might argue about what it is a symptom of.

Regan's approach offers a broadly similar way of drawing an ethical distinction between harms but, by virtue of its constraining principles, it offers a clear way out of the danger that lesser harms might be aggregated and thereby equal something truly awful. While Regan insists that **subjects–of–a–life**, such as ourselves and most mammals, are equal in terms of our **inherent value** he is not committed to the view that the experiences which we have, and the lives which we lead, are also equally valuable or rather **intrinsically valuable**. (By way of a recap, on Regan's account subjects-of-a-life have inherent value while experiences can have intrinsic value, and the latter is far less important.) Again, echoing Singer, what makes an experience intrinsically valuable is its desirability. What animals lose when their lives are taken is, in most instances, not as inherently valuable as that which humans lose. And so, Regan too is well placed to draw a significant ethical distinction between animal slaughter and the Holocaust. However, the danger of aggregating animal harm is held in check by Regan's **worse-off principle**: greater harms to any individual creature trump a larger number of lesser harms to other creatures, even when the latter harms run into millions (or, in this case, billions). This principle, which (as we have seen in Chapter 3) generates so much criticism of Regan's position, ensures that lesser harms do not aggregate and trump greater harms. And this is intuitively appealing. It explains why the treatment of the common cold, an extensively suffered malady, is a lesser priority than the treatment of rare but life-threatening illnesses. And so, although Regan himself has tended to focus on differences in the mindset of perpetrators as a reason for setting aside the Holocaust analogy, his approach does also provide a story about differences in terms of harm to the victims.

At the heart of both the Singer and the Regan approaches is an acknowledgement that humans typically (but not in all instances) do have a significantly greater interest in life. Indeed, this is at the heart of weak species egalitarianism. If the same claim can be built into a contractualist account then it too will have no difficulty in drawing an ethically significant Holocaust/slaughter distinction. (And there is no obvious reason why contractualism should be linked to any stronger version of egalitarianism.) However, this saving move simultaneously pulls animal advocacy closer in line with our everyday intuitions about the most dreadful of harms and, at the same time, it curbs the radicalism of talk about species equality. In doing so, it will fail to satisfy those animal advocates who want a stronger version of the latter, one which in practice will never *tendentially* or *systematically* privilege humans over non-humans, for whatever reason. Such a **strong species egalitarianism** may well have to commit also to the ethical equivalence of the harms involved in animal slaughter and those involved in the Holocaust, even while recognizing an ethical difference in terms of the motivation of the perpetrators. An avoidance of the Holocaust analogy will then be a matter of judgement about its political suitability. It will not be based on the idea that the analogy is itself morally reprehensible or apt to mislead.

COETZEE'S USE OF THE ANALOGY

Avoidance of the Holocaust analogy, if it is underpinned only by the pragmatic consideration that it may be politically counterproductive, has its own problems. These are captured well in a work of fiction, *Elizabeth Costello* (2003) by the author J. M. Coetzee, which has become the main shared object of attention for current discussion of the problem. While it is a work of fiction, and the analogy is deployed by one if its characters, Coetzee himself is a long-standing vegetarian who has, elsewhere, made the very same connection between animal slaughter and the Holocaust. The book tells the story of an ageing author of fiction, Elizabeth Costello, who is approaching the end of her life and has been invited to give two prestigious lectures on her own preferred topic. She chooses 'The Lives of Animals'. In the delivered lectures, she does not describe the detail of slaughter, but rather her own incredulity at our tolerance of this appalling genocide in our midst. At the customary after-lecture meal, attempts are made to shift the discussion onto the more acceptable terrain of animal rights, rather than our complicity in mass murder. Costello resists, insisting that this is not a matter of rights or even of ethical deliberation, so much as a matter of trying to save her soul. Distressing though these words may be, the reader is given to understand that she is not a religious person in any conventional sense. What she says is, rather, an attempt to capture the sense that this is not a matter about which reasonable and liberally minded moral agents can comfortably disagree with one another over a pleasant dinner. Shifting the discussion into politely acceptable discursive terms is itself taken to be a form of evasion, an evasion of the sheer awfulness of what is done and what we tolerate.

This is the Holocaust analogy taken seriously and without any trivialization of the sufferings of the victims of the Nazis. Rather, there is an elevation of the harms which are inflicted on animals rather than a levelling-down of the harms inflicted on Jews (and many others too). However, the focal point is *not* a claim about species equality any more than it is a claim about rights. This is drawn out in an episode where a Jewish academic who sends her a note explaining why he will not be breaking bread with her, in spite of the requirements of hospitality: Costello's position is morally offensive as well as wrong, it is beyond the bounds of reasonable ethical discussion. Yet, this dissenting voice is a sympathetic voice. It is the voice of the only other character who seems to share Costello's sense that these are matters of the deepest sort. They are not for the academic dinner table. Yet it really is a dissenting voice. He believes that Costello is presenting an argument to the effect that because Jews were slaughtered like animals, animals are therefore slaughtered like Jews.

Commentators, such as Cora Diamond, have suggested that this is a mistake. It involves a misunderstanding of what, in the novel, Costello is actually doing. Rather than presenting an argument about the greatness of harms, she is picturing a similarity between mechanisms of evasion. The main point is not that the appallingly inhuman harms of the Holocaust are *equal* to the appallingly inhuman harms of animal slaughter—how can one even think of applying a standard of measurement in this context? Rather, the point is that the pattern of evasion and the mechanisms of evasion are, in both cases, much the same. As bystanders, we experience a difficulty of reality—at one and the same time we know and we do not quite know what is going on. We remain in a state of ignorance which is real and yet it is a culpable ignorance. We do not seem to have learned anything at all from the greatest and most dreadful evasion of the past. And so, we are left with the impression that whether or not it is animals or humans who are slaughtered, we would respond in much the same way, given sufficient motivation to evade the truth. If this is true then anyone who avoids use of the Holocaust analogy for the merely pragmatic reason that it is impolitic may also be charged with complicity in just such a process of evasion. They may be very like a participant at a meal who wants to talk about animal rights as a substitute for talking in terms which would help us to grasp a fuller sense of the moral horror of what is done. By contrast, those who avoid the analogy because it runs too great a risk of being not just offensive but being misunderstood may find themselves on more solid ground, just so long as they do address matters in some alternative manner which attempts to capture the utter dreadfulness of what is done.

CONCLUSION

The Costello case may help us to distinguish between significantly different kinds of work that deployment of the Holocaust analogy is itself geared to accomplish. It can be used to support different sorts of claim or to picture matters in various different ways. The simplest of these is its use as a way of depicting an alarming identity of harms. This is the sense in which it is customarily understood and this is the primary source of offence: it seems to demean the harms suffered by Holocaust victims to something no greater than the loss of life by a dumb creature—a representation of matters which can also be found in at least some of the justificatory texts produced by the Nazis themselves. Secondly, the analogy can be used as a way of drawing attention to all or any one of the multiple causal and conceptual connections between animal slaughter and the Holocaust. This is the approach taken firstly by Bashevis Singer and then by Charles Patterson in his *Eternal Treblinka* (2002). For the former, our treatment of animals involves a practical commitment to the principle that 'might makes right'. Once adopted, no one is safe. The latter, while challenging our sense of superiority, does not engage in detailed value theory but rather draws out the interrelated ideas that (1) without the pre-existing techniques of the slaughterhouse, the industrialized assembly-line killing of the Holocaust would not have been practical; (2) the Nazi presentation of Jews and mental 'defectives' as subhuman, and therefore legitimately killed, would not have made any sense without a prior commitment to the legitimacy of our killing creatures who are regarded as less than human; (3) the mechanisms of partial concealment and public evasion are much the same in both cases; and finally (4) this evasion and other similarities have strikingly impressed themselves on a number of Holocaust survivors and their offspring in a way which grants at least some agents the appropriate standing to deploy the analogy.

Deployment of the analogy, even by those with the relevant family history, those best placed to deploy it, may continue to be a dangerous strategy for as long as the Holocaust remains a culturally sensitive topic. But, understood as something other than a claim of equivalent harm, it is not obvious that the analogy must always be either misleading or a source of legitimate offence. Above all, its deployment need not entail any commitment to the view that the harms which were suffered by Holocaust victims and the harms now suffered by slaughtered animals are ethically identical and therefore demanding of the same kinds of actions in response.

FURTHER READING

The most detailed development of the Holocaust analogy occurs in Charles Patterson's *Eternal Treblinka: Our Treatment of Animals and the Holocaust* (New York: Lantern Books, 2002). It contains an extended treatment of Isaac Bashevis Singer's use of the analogy across a number of stories. For a more systematic and analytic treatment of the analogy see David Sztybel's article 'Can the Treatment of Animals Be Compared to the Holocaust?', *Ethics & the Environment* 11(1) (2006): 97–132.

Coetzee's literary deployment of the Holocaust analogy can be found in *Elizabeth Costello* (London: Vintage, 2003) and *The Lives of Animals* (Princeton: Princeton University Press, 2001). For interesting philosophical engagements with this text see Stanley Cavell, Cora Diamond, John McDowell, Ian Hacking and Cary Wolfe, *Philosophy and Animal Life* (New York: Columbia University Press, 2008), and Stephen Mulhall, *The Wounded Animal: J. M. Coetzee and the Difficulty of Reality in Literature and Philosophy* (Princeton: Princeton University Press, 2008).

For the Holocaust itself, and a challenge to the idea that it was effectively hidden from view, see Daniel J. Goldhagen, *Hitler's Willing Executioners* (London: Abacus, 1997).

For a rejection of the Holocaust analogy see Raimond Gaita, *The Philosopher's Dog* (London: Routledge, 2003).

7

ABOLITIONISM

While the fracture lines within animal ethics are many and complex, the view from inside the animal rights movement, over the past two decades, has tended to prioritize a special division between supporters of what Gary Francione calls the **abolitionist** position and **new welfarism**. Francione is the leading advocate of abolitionism and argues that a call for nothing less than an end to the treatment of animals as property is the only consistent and plausible rights position available. Calls for welfare reforms which fall in any way short of the abolition of ownership and property-based practices do not, for Francione, operate within the bounds of a genuine animal rights position. They are, instead, taken to uphold the status quo. If they do so while presenting themselves as supportive of rights, or of an ultimate abolition of animal exploitation or liberation, then they are instances of new welfarism ('welfarism' for short) and constitute only a variation on the traditional theme of benevolent opposition to cruelty.

ABOLITIONISM

While familiar objections to Singer and Regan tend to hold that they go *too far*, the abolitionist position (understood in the terms set out above) holds that, as instances of welfarism, they *do not go far enough*. They adhere to what I have referred to as **weak** rather than **strong species egalitarianism**. The view that animals and humans have interests which are to be considered equally, they often do not have exactly the same interests. With regard to death, creaturely interests differ because the character of sentience also differs. Accordingly, both Singer and Regan accept that, in extreme situations, there are stable reasons prioritizing most humans over most non-humans, just so long as the rules of the prioritizing game abide by the following constraints: firstly, some ways of prioritizing must be excluded because they would be directly **speciesist** or would violate basic constraints governing cruelty and unnecessary harm; and secondly, the justification which is given for prioritizing humans over non-humans in any particular case should not appeal directly to their humanity. Instead, an appeal must be made to the fact that the human or humans in question happen to be in possession of morally salient properties such as the capacity to suffer in time-sensitive ways, the capacity to form complex desires about the future, or the capacity to exercise a special kind of autonomy—factors which may all, then, shape the extent to which death is a harm.

This may seem to secure a fair and reasonable species-neutrality; however, the properties which are taken to be especially important in such comparisons look suspiciously like they are drawn from a model of what it is like to be a normal human. If this is the case then it would seem that the special value of *typically human* properties and of *the ordinary human* is covertly presupposed as a bedrock for deliberation, with moral standing of a diminished sort then extended outwards in a controlled way. The ensuing licence to regularly prioritize humans then looks close to (and may even be) what Francione and other prominent abolitionists (notably, Joan Dunayer) have claimed, i.e. a revised form of speciesism. In a series of publications beginning with *Rain without Thunder: The Ideology of the Animal Rights Movement* (1996) Francione has charged Singer with precisely this. (His attitude towards Regan has been more conciliatory and Regan, in turn, has come to regard himself as an abolitionist, albeit of a rather different sort.)

By contrast with Singer and Regan's reassuring de facto acceptance of special human standing, the heart of Francione's abolitionism is a strong egalitarianism, one which puts humans and non-humans, figuratively, down on all fours with each other as sentient beings.

On such an approach, there is no reason to privilege the way in which cognitively normal humans experience the world. Sentience matters, but our kind of sentience turns out to be nothing special. Accordingly, even in the absence of complex (time-sensitive) patterns of desire, preference and anticipation, the loss of an animal life *may* be just as great a harm to the animal as the loss of a human life would be to a human. With regard to Regan's notoriously problematic dog-in-a-lifeboat situation (imagined scenarios where we have to decide between saving a human and saving one or many dogs) Francione accepts that we will *sometimes* have reasons to decide in favour of the human. Sometimes, all that we may have to fall back on is the merely epistemic consideration that we happen to know what it is like to be a human but we do not know what it is like to be a dog. However, at other times we may just as readily have reasons to decide in favour of the dog. There may, for example, be an extremely old human in the boat (a thought which might draw out a charge of age-based prejudice or 'ageism'). Moreover, this need not be an exceptional circumstance. For the abolitionist or, again, the abolitionist in Francione's sense, there is no general rule which will allow an animal rights advocate to reassure the everyday speciesist that human interests will generally (if covertly) retain their special, privileged standing.

This takes Francione off in a quite different direction from the first-wave animal liberation theories of Singer and Regan. While both of the latter have persistently argued for the **moral considerability** of animals by appeal to ways in which they are similar to us (*they too* can suffer, *they too* are subjects of a life) Francione's position is based on the view that animal minds do not have to be approximations to human minds in order for us to assert that animals and humans have equal moral standing. All that is required for moral standing is sentience (of whatever sort) and, for Francione, all creatures which happen to have moral standing have it *equally*.

The latter claim, a version of strong species egalitarianism which appeals to the equal significance of all sentience, is more controversial than the idea that sentience grants standing *of some sort* or *to some degree*. It will also generate counter-intuitive consequences if sentience is attributed to a broad range of non-human creatures, not just livestock, cats and dogs but also fish and even insects. (And here we might do well to bear in mind the fact that vegetarians and vegans will no more eat insects than they would eat cattle. Indeed, vegan organizations but not all vegans tend to regard honey as analogous to dairy and therefore off-limits.) If we adhere to strict sentience egalitarianism the growing body of evidence for sentience in wasps and bees, together with the evidence of sensitivity to pain in fish, will then imply that they too have *equal* moral standing with humans. There are three main difficulties with this position. The first is that it probably qualifies as a 'fearless thought', in the sense treated already as problematic, i.e. a conclusion which is so radically in conflict with deeply embedded intuitions that it might reasonably be taken as a *reductio ad absurdum*, an indication that one or more of the assumptions from which it is derived must be wrong.

The second problem is that it may prove too much. If true, it could impact disastrously on the case for veganism given the extent of insect death which is an unavoidable aspect of the harvesting of cereal crops. Standard responses to the harvesting problem—to the effect that the deaths in question are inadvertent—tend to presuppose that the insects which are killed are either of less importance than livestock animals *or else* that they are harmed in a lesser manner than livestock would be by slaughter. Were this not the case, a replacement of cereal consumption with the consumption of grass-fed cattle (but not cereal-fed cattle) would be the best way to minimize harm.

The final problem is that it is difficult to see how such a standpoint could actually be inhabited by humans in general rather than adopted as a special kind of religious commitment adhered to by a small cluster of individuals living a dedicated religious life, a life akin to the Jainism which Francione acknowledges as a key influence on his thought. However, it is Joan Dunayer, in *Speciesism* (2004), who has pressed sentience egalitarianism, and the moral standing of creatures such as insects, furthest. Francione has, instead, been cautious about explicit commitment. His attitude is qualified as precautionary: we should treat creatures as sentient unless and until we find out otherwise.

Given the counter-intuitive nature of such a strict sentience egalitarianism we may wonder whether it might be better to suggest that there is a threshold of sentience which both humans and a more restricted range of other creatures (cats, dogs and primates, and so on) have crossed which gives us (in an extended sense) special standing. For any creature which crosses it a significant *and* equal moral standing might then be accepted. However, the difficulty with this intuition-saving move is that it would presumably be based on an appeal to the differing interests (or to something akin to the latter) which go with differing levels of sentience. If accepted, it would then be rather difficult to prevent any further contrasts being drawn between the interests which go with normal human sentience, and the interests which go with the kinds of sentience that cats, dogs and cows or pigs generally have. And this is precisely what Francione wishes to avoid.

Apart from **sentientism** (a basing of value on the sheer capacity for experience) and **strong species egalitarianism**, the abolitionist position also entails the disturbing idea that acceptance of the treatment of animals as property is no more justified than the toleration of the great wrongs of human history. However, the paradigmatic wrong which is appealed to as analogous is not the Holocaust but slavery. As with the **Holocaust analogy**, this **slavery analogy** should not only be disturbing to meat-eaters, it should also be disturbing to many, and perhaps most, vegans and vegetarians. If there is a moral equivalent to the slave system in our midst then few of us can reasonably claim to have done enough to oppose it, expose it and bring it down. And here the point is not simply that we fall short (a simple point about our being ethically less than perfect). Rather, the point is that we fall short in a matter which is severe but which can also be addressed. Disturbing though this thought may be, abolitionists have pressed the slavery analogy in a way which has made it into a key feature of the abolitionist standpoint. It is the principal analogy which they use to emphasize the importance of targeting the property status of animals. Ideas of liberation and talk about rights, which have often been rather vague, are, with the help of the slavery analogy, distilled into the call for an end to animals being held as property. Without an end to animals as property, abolitionists such as Francione believe that *all* rights attributions will be meaningless because they may be overruled in favour of even the most trivial human interests (such as culinary preference).

COMBINING ETHICS AND POLITICAL STRATEGY

This forceful and, in a sense, uncompromising critique of the first-wave theories of Singer and Regan has had a major impact on the actual direction of (and justifications offered for) contemporary animal rights activism. A significant section of the animal rights movement has come to regard abolitionism, with qualification, as a suitable replacement theory. Others have come to accept that a replacement theory or new orthodoxy is required but deny that abolitionism fits the bill. Organizational divisions have ensued with pressure on activist groupings to nail their colours to the mast and come out for or against the abolitionist standpoint. Yet it is not immediately obvious that prominent groupings which have come to label themselves as abolitionist (such as the Australian organizations which have pioneered **open rescue** at poultry farms) actually abide by the rules of engagement which Francione would regard as falling strictly within abolitionist bounds. Indeed, the pressure on activists to target welfare reforms, as part of an incremental pathway to abolition, remains considerable. (For more on open rescue, see Chapter 9.)

It may then be tempting to suggest that abolitionism is good ethics but bad politics. That it is simply impractical when compared with what it seeks to replace. Such a move might, however, be rather too hasty. At the level of theorizing animal ethics, the emergence of abolitionism has performed at least one important function which has been widely accepted as legitimate and which is likely to shape any plausible successor theory to Singer and Regan. Abolitionism has promoted a tight connection between animal ethics and political strategy. Whereas Singer and Regan set their ethical goals (an end to various forms of exploitative animal use) but left issues of political strategy open-ended (albeit with a pre-supposition in favour of welfare reforms), Francione's critique has fused together its conception of an appropriate goal and its conception of the appropriate means. This has been a persuasive move for animal ethicists who are otherwise sceptical about any form of strict abolitionism.

Even well-known critics such as Robert Garner and Alasdair Cochrane have tended to accept that a closer, or more explicit, fusion of the ethical and the political is the right way to go. The rationale for making this move is straightforward. It involves nothing more controversial than the endorsement of an '*ought*' implies '*can*' position. If calls for either **animal liberation** or some extensive system of animal rights are to be meaningful then there must be a way in which the relevant goal or goals could actually be brought about. If we *ought* to adopt a particular end goal which is fixed by ethical deliberation then we should satisfy ourselves that there is a political means whereby it *can* be achieved. Without the latter, the former will be vacuous.

Such agreement over the need for a closer and/or more explicit fusion of animal ethics and politics does not, however, bridge the gulf between the rival positions about the actual political strategy which is appropriate and, more specifically, it does not bridge the gulf between abolitionists and their critics over the question of what is to be done while radical change (up to and including abolition) remains a long way off. Critics suggest that while abolitionists have highlighted the importance of political strategy they themselves lack one. Or, more precisely, the charge is that abolitionists lack a coherent and plausible strategy for the here and now. Francione's reply to this charge has remained much the same since the 1990s: the only meaningful overall progress for the time being is an expansion of the abolitionist political constituency through the growth of veganism (vegetarianism being regarded by abolitionists as too complicit in animal harms, indeed *just as* complicit as meat-eating).

While it has frequently been suggested that this response under-estimates the ethical merits of vegetarianism, misses its role as a bridge to veganism and overstates the vegan/vegetarian separation, the vegan outreach work of abolitionists is, in at least one respect, uncontroversial. Generally, the attitude of animal rights advocates (of whatever hue) is that veganism is a good idea and the more vegans there are, the better the world will be. It is also difficult to envisage any positive and fundamental change in human/animal relations without a prior and significant expansion of the numbers of those who consume a non-meat diet and do so for ethical reasons. There is also some evidence that veganism *could* be grown more rapidly if the relevant kinds of institutional support were in place. (Organizations such as the Vegan Society in the UK receive more pledges to try veganism than they can cope with.) However, it has been suggested (by the long-standing activist Kim Stallwood among others) that a focus on vegan outreach at the expense of political lobbying, and campaigns over particular instances of animal abuse, can give activists the impression that they are part of a moral crusade rather than a genuine political movement.

While it has been repeatedly charged that abolitionists place too much exclusive weight on vegan outreach work, it is the abolitionist hostility to campaigns over animal welfare as pointless or counter-productive which is the main source of controversy among rights advocates. For the abolitionist, or at least the strict abolitionist who adheres closely to Francione, welfare campaigning remains akin to (or simply *is*) the finding of less disturbing ways to use and exploit. In support of this, abolitionists point to the way in which meat producers have received praise from welfare-oriented activists when such producers have adopted some modified form of animal harm. A prominent example is the public praise from PETA (the US-based People for the Ethical Treatment of Animals) for various industry reforms instituted in the aftermath of the lengthy 'McLibel' court case. In the 1990s McDonald's sued two animal rights protestors for publicizing claims about production methods used by the food chain's suppliers. The case was to run for years and involved a stream of bad publicity which McDonald's had not anticipated. The resulting investigations into the actual practices of suppliers did not confirm all of the protestors' disputed claims but it did disclose a number of practices which both the courts and senior management at McDonald's found shocking and/or likely to be commercially damaging. The upshot was a tightening of welfare standards. Temple Grandin was brought in to redesign the slaughterhouse system, with a view towards reducing animal stress and the number of cattle who went under the knife while still conscious. (Grandin was quick to point out the cost of delays whenever animals became stressed and non-compliant.) PETA's public, if qualified, praise for Grandin's work was regarded by some as a readiness to make reasonable pragmatic compromises but it also lent plausibility to Francione's charge that welfare campaigning could legitimate slaughter in the eyes of the broader public.

While Francione points to the example of PETA as a warning about the dangers of welfarism, critics have tended to point to other examples which show abolitionism in a far less favourable light. Proposition 2 in California is a case in point. In 2008 an amendment to state law was voted on in California, a move to abolish various forms of animal confinement in sow stalls, veal crates and battery cages. It was proposed that the animals must have sufficient room to lie down, stand up and extend their limbs fully (with exceptions for transportation and various other activities such as veterinary research and rodeos). Because the legislation presupposed the continuation of animal use albeit under improved conditions, Francione opposed Proposition 2 and did so publicly. The move opened abolitionists up to a charge of putting political ideology and their own doctrinal purity before the interests of actually existing fellow creatures, all of whom were liable to be dead long before abolition arrived (if it ever did).

Such a charge might well be warranted if the dominant target of abolitionist criticism was actual *welfare reform* rather than *campaigning for welfare reform*. While there is often some slippage between the two, Francione's own intervention over Proposition 2 might seem to be atypical. Generally, his target is the latter and not the former. Indeed, his position is often attacked as a contribution to internecine, internal disputes rather than having any real friction with the world. Francione's response to the charge that he puts ideology before animal interests has been to challenge the extent and significance of the welfare changes which have actually been implemented and to assert that welfare changes *will* happen with or without activist support for them. They will occur for purely commercial reasons because reforms promote a more efficient exploitation. Activists should not, therefore, expend their limited resources and energies doing the meat industry's job for it. Such changes will occur with or without activist intervention. Such a response, again, indicates that the dominant focus of Francione's criticism is welfare campaigning rather than welfare reforms themselves. We might then have to look to the world and see how welfare change occurs before endorsing the charge of the critics.

THE APPEAL OF ABOLITIONISM

What has motivated the abolitionist position, particularly in the US, has been a perceived lack of apparent progress towards any of the major goals which, since the 1970s, animal rights activists have prioritized: an end to animal experimentation, industrialized meat production and activities such as hunting. It might even be thought that Francione speaks to a sense of impatience or even disillusion-ment among activists. In part, this may be true. However, the story is not entirely straightforward. Outside of the US, especially in Europe, there *have* been all manner of partial exceptions which look like real, if limited, forms of progress. Following years of campaigning, there has been a ban on fox hunting in the UK, although it has not been consistently enforced or favourably interpreted in the courts; there has been a ban on bullfighting in Catalonia (but not the rest of Spain); and a wider ban on animal testing for cosmetics is currently being rolled out, in protracted stages, across the entire European Union. Opponents of Francione have been quick to suggest that his brand of abolitionism is a response to US conditions which ignores the rather more effective mechanisms of regulation which operate in Europe and that he has underplayed comparable, if localized, US successes such as Proposition 2.

In a published, co-edited debate with Francione, Robert Garner has pointed to the fact that in the US a more liberal economic ideal prevails, one which does make incremental regulative progress of any sort harder to secure and often less dramatic when it arrives. In line with this, we might expect that as a response to the European ban on cosmetics testing, a similar US ban may, at some time, reluctantly be accepted if only to secure continued market access and penetration. But it is notable that the US tends to follow while the more media-noted gains originate elsewhere. To this it might also be added that the proportion of vegans to vegetarians in the US also happens to be unusually high, higher than in Europe or Australia. And this too may operate as a 'push' factor which makes the direct route of building veganism seem more attractive in the US than elsewhere. The upshot is that strict abolitionism is primarily a US and Internet phenomenon. What activists mean when they call themselves 'abolitionists' in Europe and elsewhere (Australia again being the obvious example) is often something rather different and significantly less hostile to welfare campaigning.

Even so, while supporters of welfare reform point to localized US successes such as Proposition 2 and to events in Europe, abolitionists (of the stricter sort) have tended to follow Francione by playing down claimed regulative successes wherever they occur. When formulated with insufficient caution, this can make abolitionism seem like a form of denial, a refusal to accept the sheer facts of the matter. Yet there is an argumentative response available to the abolitionist which, to some extent, defuses the significance of localized successes by stressing instead the *overall* situation, the bigger picture, which *is* one of a steady increase in animal consumption and use.

It is not simply that progress towards an ending of animal exploitation and harm is uncomfortably slow. Rather, a massive increase has occurred in the main forms of animal use over the past three decades. While there is a widespread *belief*, outside the ranks of animal rights activists, that things are getting better, that we now treat animals more humanely, matters have numerically become far worse. Animal slaughter is practised without some of the more appalling historical methods (without, for example, dispatching by hammer on a killing floor) but slaughter is more extensive now than at any other time in human history. And with scale has come animal concentration, removal from pastures and heavy dosing with antibiotics. The abolitionist who points to this, rather than denying various localized improvements in particular aspects of the treatment of particular groups of animals, will have a strong case. However, abolitionists are reluctant to make the move, precisely because it may seem to highlight the relative advantages of ethically informed animal farming.

Nonetheless, understanding the problem of extent, of quantitative increase, is key to grasping the seriousness of the charge that Francione makes when he asserts that those who campaign for incremental welfare changes are sustaining an illusion of progress. Whatever else he is doing, he is not *simply* refusing to face the facts. Rather, Francione is focusing attention on a different set of facts. However, the suggestion that welfarists (of whatever shade or hue) actually, in some general way, help to sustain an illusion of progress is difficult to establish. It is difficult to envisage what the effective mechanism for this might be, given that the charge presupposes more of an impact than any group of animal rights activists can reasonably claim to have had on *overall* popular perceptions of animal harm. It is, for example, not at all obvious that animal rights activists have shaped, or in any way dramatically shifted, public perceptions of the overall treatment of animals at any time since the 1970s when exposés of laboratory experimentation hit the headlines. There are some exceptions, such as the work of open rescue activists in Australia, who have managed, to a degree, to shape public perceptions of egg production and poultry farming through much the same technique of media exposé. But beyond this, the animal rights movement remains too small to have any great or even clear role in shaping overall perceptions of animal treatment and misfortunes. Indeed, the dominant view of animal rights supporters is that they are extremists who will never be satisfied by even the most reasonable reforms. Among the public at large there simply is no perception of any difference at all between welfarists and abolitionists. These are 'insider' terms.

This is not, however, to suggest political irrelevance as opposed to the fact that the animal rights movement is still only just emerging as a political force (just as it took decades for the ecology movement to emerge as a significant force). The incremental growth of vegetarianism and veganism in both Europe and the US may well suggest that the animal rights movement will eventually have its day. It will eventually have an impact of some stable and lasting sort. But, for the present, as either a political movement or as a moral crusade, it has yet to attain the critical mass required to shape popular perceptions about the overall treatment of animals. Although the US has a larger than usual ratio of vegans to vegetarians, the levels of vegetarianism and veganism combined are still below 5 per cent in the US, Europe and even Australia. Depending on which figures we trust, the true level probably sits somewhere closer to 3 per cent and most of the latter will qualify as welfarists by Francione's criteria. (Abolitionism is, again, more of an activist standpoint and most vegetarians and vegans are not activists.) If we are to explain why so many people, perhaps even a majority, hold to the mistaken belief that our overall humane treatment of animals is improving then we should probably look to the media, industry, political structures, received practice and a certain psychological evasiveness that we are all subject to. If these considerations are irrelevant to the charge of sustaining illusions— because the charge does not concern the overall patterning of public perceptions but rather some more localized impact—then it is not clear exactly *who* is being effectively misled by welfarists, given that many of the latter explicitly qualify their acknowledgement of reforms.

The charge of promoting illusion is not, however, Francione's only criticism of welfarism. He has a number of subsidiary charges, the most prominent of which are the following. Firstly, those welfarists who hope for liberation through incremental welfare reform either have no real strategy (they are just hoping that things will work out) or else they are committed to a flawed strategy of economic attrition against meat-eating. They believe that a steady diminution of the practice may be brought about through the raising of costs of production. In short, products which involve animal harm and mistreatment can be made too expensive to produce and to consume on anything like the current scale. There is a thought here that many welfarists may entertain, the thought that industry can be made to shift by the application of economic pressure. And so, for example, the animal-testing ban on cosmetics produced in Europe *is* likely to exert at least some pressure in the US. However, the precise strategy which Francione outlines as typical of welfarism clearly *is* a flawed strategy. As he has been quick to point out, welfare reforms such as Temple Grandin's redesigning of slaughterhouses do put some producers out of business but they can also introduce overall efficiencies as the industry standard. However, it is not at all obvious that support for incremental welfare reforms has any necessary or regular connection to such a strategy. Indeed, as noted above, the main first-wave positions which Francione regards as implicated in welfarism were broadly supportive of incremental changes, but also strategy-neutral. Economic attrition is one option among others but not the one which is most obviously favoured. The dominant attitude among supporters of welfare who have some overall strategic direction is the use of welfare campaigns as both a means of successive legislative constraint and as a means of growing the political constituency for further restriction.

Secondly, Francione argues that by backing one regime of animal exploitation against another, in the manner typical of praising certain forms of traditional farming, welfarists become complicit in the continuation of animal use. A problem here is that, setting aside extreme cases (exemplified by PETA's praise for Temple Grandin), preferring a more-constrained wrong over a less-constrained one does not obviously require or imply actual *approval* of wrongdoing. Comparisons have often been made here with the traditional attitude of Marxists towards trade union activism and industrial militancy. The latter operates clearly within the bounds of capitalism and negotiation of the terms on which labour is exploited by capital. Yet few people have regarded the support of Marxists for militant trade unionism as, in any way, an actual endorsement of, or prop for, capitalism. (Some anarchists might be an exception here but anarchism too has a strong tradition of industrial militancy for economic amelioration.) The operative point here is that opposition to exploitation does not in any obvious way entail neutrality about the terms on which exploitation persists while it continues to do so. Abolitionism then appears to be analogous not simply to support for revolutionary change, but to a politically naive ultra-leftism of a sort which has been attacked by all of the figures on the left who have had the most political impact (such as Lenin who, rather unkindly, referred to the rejection of campaigns for reform as an 'infantile disorder').

Francione has, however, challenged the value of this analogy and there may be some grounds for thinking that a different one might be a better fit (not least, the fact that Marxism has, to date, failed in the West—a consideration which makes it a rather poor model for future political practice). There are, however, other candidate political movements which offer a better analogue. One of the latter is the anti-abortion movement. In both the US and the UK their dominant strategy has been to go for incremental constraint on abortion through a focus on time limits. This has required anti-abortionists to support legislation which actually permits abortion in a reduced number of cases. Typically, anti-abortionists have provided the relevant support and then moved the focus of their campaigning on to a call for even tighter constraints. Such an approach has allowed the anti-abortion movement to punch well above its weight, given that support for its overall goals has never been significantly higher than 10–20 per cent of the population. But it has not led to any public confusion about whether or not anti-abortionists approve of abortion. Prominent individuals take every opportunity to make their ultimate objective clear through qualifications of the following sort: 'I oppose all abortion but if it is to continue then it is better that there be fewer abortions rather than more.' This does not seem to involve complicity other than that which is a matter of political necessity, given the nature and structure of our existing liberal democratic institutions. It seems, rather, to involve preferring what anti-abortionists see as a less extensive evil to a more extensive one.

Finally, Francione has added the subsidiary charge that welfarism is linked, not simply to misdirection, but to institutional misdirection. Large organizations such as PETA need a steady flow of funds in order to keep going. To secure such funds they need at least some claimed successes. To secure these successes they need to target achievable objectives even if the objectives have no relevance to the ultimate abolition of animal use or to the treatment of animals as property. They also need to play up the image of success and of overall progress. This charge echoes similar criticisms of the larger ecology organizations (such as Greenpeace and Friends of the Earth) which have been made by groupings with a more militant orientation (such as Earth First and the Sea Shepherds). While it may contain several grains of truth, the charge is effective primarily as an attack on the institutionalization of activism rather than effective as an attack on the very idea of linking limited gains to ultimate objectives (in the present case, linking welfare reform to animal liberation up to and including the abolition of animals as property).

TENSIONS WITHIN ABOLITIONISM

While abolitionism may seem to offer a clear separation from any taint of complicity with animal use it does not escape from all inner tensions. Not all welfare reforms involve the *mere* modification of an exploitative or abusive practice. Instead, some reforms involve the ending (i.e. the abolition) of a particular practice. Examples here would be the ending of primate use in experimentation, the capture of animals for use in zoos, or the use of any animals whatsoever for cosmetics research. Campaigns over such issues have divided the leading abolitionists even to the point where Francione's authority (which abolitionsts are already, in some cases, uncomfortable about) has been placed in question. He has, in the past, supported particular abolitionist campaigns albeit hesitantly. An example is the Great Ape Project (1993), a campaign which originated in a book of the same name and in an associated declaration which briefly brought together Singer, Francione and Regan in a call for the ending of primate harms. Francione subsequently withdrew his support, expressing regret for involvement. The grounds for regret were twofold. Even though it called for the end of a practice and not its modification, from a stricter abolitionist point of view it seemed to privilege the importance of one kind of creature, one with close human connections, over others. Moreover, any success in this one area (which for Francione has no *special* importance) might reinforce the illusion of overall progress just as readily as the mere reform of some other practice. If welfarist reforms risk sustaining the illusion of progress it is difficult to see how abolitionist reforms could avoid doing so, given that the public at large simply do not differentiate between the two.

The upshot of this difficulty of situating isolated abolitionist measures, and of single-issue campaigns in favour of them, has been a tension within abolitionist ranks. Over the years, Francione has become increasingly uneasy about any form of single-issue campaigning and comfortable only when placing emphasis on vegan outreach. To some extent this shift may be a response to pressure generated by Joan Dunayer's presentation of a purer or stricter form of abolitionism in which all legitimate campaigns have to meet stringently abolitionist criteria, beyond merely ending a practice, in order to qualify as genuinely abolitionist. This emphasis on stringency has had an unexpected side effect. Tom Regan has come to occupy some of the territory vacated by Francione by embracing an incrementalist abolitionism with a strong focus on abolitionist single-issue campaigns and a far less restrictive conception of what it takes for any particular campaign to be abolitionist. This still leaves concerns over abolitionist responses to non-abolitionist measures (such as Proposition 2) but it has the merit of combining vegan outreach work with actual activism which is, more or less, the stable combination of behaviours which has characterized the modern animal rights movement since its emergence in the 1970s. By contrast, stricter forms of abolitionism risk placing themselves at a distance from activist practice.

Given the emergence of variant forms of abolitionism, represented by Francione, Dunayer and Regan, we may begin to wonder about just how far the concept can be stretched and whether the contrast with welfarism is quite as useful and informative as it initially seemed to be when Francione first began to publish. It may, for example, be unduly restrictive to exclude Regan's incrementalist abolitionism. What appears to be excluded is only an incrementalism which is prepared to endorse non-abolitionist welfare measures (for whatever reason). But here it may still seem unhelpful to exclude consideration of the reasons for such endorsements, given that many of those who do endorse them do so alongside, and even in the name of, a claimed ultimate commitment to abolition. Given such a claimed commitment to abolition, it may again seem ungenerous (unhelpful too) to label those who hold to such a standpoint as mere welfarists. A purely strategic division about *means* should not, after all, be represented as a disagreement about *ends* unless it genuinely entails such a disagreement (and this is something which would be difficult to show).

Faced with such a challenge to the contrast, an abolitionist (at least in Francione's sense) will no doubt respond by pointing out that anyone who goes around supporting exactly the same campaigns as dyed-in-the-wool welfarists (who have absolutely no further commitment to abolition) is, *in every practical sense that matters*, also a welfarist. (The pragmatist saying that 'there can be no difference anywhere that doesn't make a difference elsewhere' springs readily to mind.) This may be a sobering thought, one which may lead activists who, in theory at least, support the abolition of animal use, to reflect critically on exactly what does differentiate them in a practical way from well-meaning opponents of animal cruelty who lack any further and more radical objective.

THE ANALOGY WITH SLAVERY

Not only has the appropriateness of Francione's way of drawing a line between abolitionists and welfarists been brought into question, so too has the significance which abolitionists attribute to the standing of animals as property and to the analogy between the predicament of domesticated animals and that of slaves. Again, for obvious reasons connected to the plantation system, the civil rights movement and patterns of urban dissent over alleged institutional racism within police forces, this is an analogy which may have greater resonance in the US than it does in Europe or elsewhere. While it is an analogy which can stand alone, independently of commitment to abolitionism of any sort, it has nonetheless been placed at the heart of all the main articulations of abolitionism because of the way in which it highlights the issue of property rights. Francione and others are clearest in their rejection of any campaigning for welfare reforms which leave animals with the standing of mere property. The claim of the abolitionist (again in Francione's sense) is that while animals are regarded as instances of the latter they simply *cannot* have rights in any meaningful sense. To be property is, after all, to be a *thing* and in the eyes of the law *things* simply do not have rights.

This reading of the property standing of animals is not a point on which the abolitionist case has fared particularly well. To many critics, it radically underestimates the flexibility or open texture of the concept of property. If, for example, I own a historic building I cannot do whatever I want with it. Similarly, if I own a run-down tenement, I may be subject to some manner of improvement or demolition order. Even if I act with due diligence, I may be subject to a compulsory purchase order. An absolute conception of property ownership, as an entitlement of the owning agent to do whatever she likes with a mere thing, looks like it has little connection to actual legal practice. And, in the context of animals, the constraints to which property is subject can be based on various considerations, including the fact that the property in question is *not* merely a thing but a sentient being of some sort. This is why the assignment of family pets in divorce cases is sometimes regarded as a custody issue, while the possession of wardrobes is not. In recognition of the qualified nature of property ownership, we can also make better sense of the wide range of institutions of human slavery which have existed at different places and at different times, some of which accorded far more standing to slaves than others. Such standing has included rights of sanctuary, rights of manumission after a certain number of years and rights which go with administrative roles.

The animal/slave analogy has also proven to be similarly problematic. Although on this matter, abolitionists have tended to give more ground. There are, after all, various respects in which the predicament of slaves and domesticated animals clearly differ. Abolitionists are not entirely blind to this fact. Firstly, slaves can bring about their own liberation, while animals cannot. The burgeoning mass of slaves in the antebellum South was itself an important political liability which threatened the political institutions of the South and generated pressure to secure unqualified legislative approval for slavery from federal institutions. The massive expansion of animal breeding for use has, by contrast, in no way undermined animal use or brought in its wake a threat of self-emancipation. Nor will it ever do so. At least some animals may exercise agency, there may even be some senses in which they might be regarded as political agents, but they could never threaten insurrection or join an opposing army. Secondly, domesticated animals are for the most part bred for consumption or companionship and not for a life of labour. Human slavery, by contrast, has generally been inseparable from the binding not just of individual beings but of a workforce. And this is a situation which standardly generates opportunities for organized collective dissent with a capacity both to secure welfare concessions from owners and to bring servile grievances to the attention of the non-servile public.

Finally, because the dependence of domesticated animals on humans is entrenched, there is (in most cases) no real prospect that they might enjoy a good and fully independent life *after* liberation or *after* the abolition of their standing as property. It is for this reason that abolitionists (at least in the Francione sense) tend to support **extinctionism**, i.e. the cessation of creaturely dependence by rendering the relevant types of animals extinct. For the extinctionist, new domesticated animals are not to be brought into existence. This applies not only to livestock but also to pets. Abolition is not, therefore, regarded as a road to freedom in quite the way that it was for slaves in the US. Rather it is viewed as a road to extinction.

This prospect raises a number of ethical concerns one of which is the worry that we should not be driving species, or even specialized lineages, into actual extinction unless there is some dreadful physiological problem with the species or lineage, one which involves ongoing physical distress. Another is that extinctionism reduces animal rights, at least in the case of domesticated creatures, to being primarily (or exclusively) negative. The only right which seems to matter is a right not to be treated as someone's property. Human rights, by contrast, involve all sorts of positive entitlements which are part and parcel of individual and political liberty. The animal rights position, when understood in abolitionist terms, then begins to look rather thin and perhaps also speciesist in the sense that *we* end up with a broad range of **positive rights** but *they* do not. The option of avoiding this by thinning out our conception of human rights also seems unappealing. Given this, any plausible (if partial) bridging of the gulf between animal standing and the standing of humans may entail a rejection of extinctionism and hence of familiar variants of abolitionism. A prominent way of trying to make such a bridging move, in recent years, has been through a discussion about whether or not animals can be regarded as citizens or as, in some way, *analogous to* citizens of their own territorially established communities or of a mixed human/non-human community. Indeed, the latter move is motivated by a rejection of the extinctionist standpoint.

However, even if concern about the thinness of extinctionist conceptions of rights could be addressed there would still be an obvious ethical difficulty with extinctionism. Animals cannot be persuaded into sexual abstinence. If there are to be no further generations of dependent creatures then this can only be brought about through forms of coercion which are typified by neutering, i.e. by a physical seizure of the bodies of animals in order to make them conform to our human plans. It is difficult to see how this could ever be legitimated without at the same time legitimating various forms of benevolent human control such as those which are typical of pet ownership or (in the revised terminology) animal guardianship.

Considerations of the sort just outlined suggest that 'abolition', as it is conceived of by Francione, Dunayer and other strict abolitionists, has only a partial connection to *abolition* in the sense in play for the nineteenth-century movement against slavery. Similarly, the analogy with slavery is, at best, somewhat loose. Even so, as a point in their favour, abolitionists do not need to press the analogy too far in order for it to perform at least one important and perhaps useful function. It has been used to shift attention away from the more disturbing analogy which was previously in danger of becoming dominant, the analogy between animal slaughter and the Holocaust. This is an analogy which has been regarded by many commentators as both misleading and morally offensive. Furthermore, it may be problematic to press the *disanalogies* between human slavery and animal ownership too far. As we shall see in Chapter 9, attempts to construct an interest-based account of animal rights beyond the **negative rights** which abolitionists focus on have involved the claim that most animals have little or no direct interest in liberty. On the strongest version of this claim, presented by Alasdair Cochrane, while a domesticated animal will have an interest in freedom from a cruel owner it will have no interest in freedom as such. At the very least, this position runs contrary to the intuition that *being owned* is already to have one's moral standing not erased but compromised in significant respects. If abolitionism can claim to have a central accomplishment, it is the theory's success in directing our attention to this fact.

CONCLUSION

Abolitionism has played a major role in directing attention to the question of which ultimate ends ought to be pursued. By contrast, the first-wave approaches of Singer and Regan were far less precise about what, if any, future we humans and other non-humans might have together. Relatedly, abolitionism has helped to bring about a political turn in which questions of political agency, and how to make progress towards ethical goals, have received more direct attention. The strategy-neutrality of first-wave theories has given way. However, any claim that abolitionism presents a viable overall successor theory to the first-wave approaches will be more problematic. Abolitionism has generated its own set of problems, only some of which concern the disputed impact of welfare campaigns. Its endorsements of sentience egalitarianism and extinctionism have also led to significant challenges. While sentience egalitarianism which goes *all the way down* to insects seems to be the most consistent articulation of abolitionism, it is also deeply implausible and, if embraced, might generate unwelcome consequences for the practice of veganism. Similarly, extinctionism, because it yields an extremely thin conception of animal rights (at least in the case of domesticated creatures), may inadvertently reintroduce a form of species prejudice, given the wide range of positive rights which are standardly ascribed to humans.

FURTHER READING

Joan Dunayer's *Speciesism* (Derwood, MD: Ryce Publications, 2004) together with the following texts by Gary Francione are the main statements of abolitionism: *Rain without Thunder: The Ideology of the Animal Rights Movement* (Philadelphia, PA: Temple University Press, 1996); *Introduction to Animal Rights: Your Child or the Dog* (Philadelphia, PA: Temple University Press, 2000); *Animals as Persons* (New York: Columbia University Press, 2008); and (with Robert Garner) *The Animal Rights Debate* (New York: Columbia University Press, 2010). For an interview where Tom Regan explains his incrementalist version of abolitionism see 'The Tom Regan Week: On Achieving Abolitionist Goals', *Animal Rights Zone* [blog], posted 18 May 2011, <http://arzone.ning.com/forum/topics/the-tom-regan-week-on? xg_source=activity>. For criticism of Francione's account of the property status of animals, see Alasdair Cochrane, *Animal Rights without Liberation* (New York: Columbia University Press, 2012), 148–53. For a classic comparison between animals and slaves, see Yi-Fu Tuan's *Dominance and Affection: The Making of Pets* (New Haven: Yale University Press, 1984). For the McLibel case and its aftermath see Peter Singer and Jim Mason, *Eating: What We Eat and Why It Matters* (London: Arrow Books, 2006), 69–76.

8

ANIMALS AND THE
ENVIRONMENT

If we were to set out a series of the most basic ethical requirements for human/animal relations, one of these requirements would be that cruelty should be avoided and that due regard should be given to animal interests. Acknowledging this much will commit us to tackling the familiar issues of animal welfare in line with one of the most fundamental liberal constraints. On any plausible account of cruelty-free welfare, animals should not be kept in crates, they should not be kicked and abused by humans who are supposed to be caring for them, and they should also not be mutilated for human convenience: their beaks should not be seared off, healthy parts of their bodies (such as tails) should not be amputated, and so on. A further basic requirement for human/animal relations is that more detailed rules governing the treatment of animals should not conflict too greatly or directly with our broader liberal norms concerning tolerance and respect for freedom. This can be conceived of as either a requirement which we may embrace or concede as a matter of realpolitik. We live in broadly liberal societies, are likely to continue to do so, and (with regard to animals) this may be advantageous. Once certain mythologies about more authoritarian systems are stripped away, the known alternatives to liberal democracy have not offered adequate ways to address animal needs and interests.

So far, the requirements have been linked directly to liberal norms. A further requirement has a more naturalistic character: our relations with animals should be ecologically viable. Any way of acting which results in systematic damage to the environment will be extremely difficult to defend. An ecologically unviable approach towards animal ethics might, of course, be well intentioned but it would also be counterproductive. Without suitable environmental safeguards, future generations of both humans and animals will suffer, the planet will suffer and perhaps we will suffer also.

Individually, these three requirements or basic 'adequacy conditions' for any animal ethic, each appear solid, but getting all three to harmonize may be somewhat harder. What we often find is that **animal advocates** tend to stress one of these requirements as if it were primary or able to do all of the work. The third requirement, ecological sustainability, is a popular choice. Our industrialized food systems, meat production on an inconceivably vast scale, cause massive amounts of ecological harm. Imagine an enormous gathering of animals, stretching out into millions in every direction, perhaps as far as the eye can see. Imagine a system in which this many animals are killed and processed every single day without exception, a system in which several hundred times more animals are continuously fed and reared to take their place. Such a system, driven by short-term profit rather than environmental impact, could have a devastating impact on planetary ecology. And that is precisely what seems to be happening.

It is frequently, and perhaps correctly, pointed out that there is no obvious way to modify or to reform such practices which would render them neutral, or even sustainable. Mass, industrialized livestock rearing comes also at the price of unavoidable cruelty as individual creatures are subjected to, or simply lost in, huge systems of time-sensitive production, where stopping the production line to ensure that all animals are unconscious when processed is simply not an option. These matters are a point of agreement between animal advocates and supporters of best-practice meat-eating who, by and large, tend to favour smallholding, grass farming and traditional rearing techniques as opposed to the industrialized system. Insofar as we can think ourselves into the animal's point of view, the former seems definitely preferable to the latter. This ecologically based critique of industrialized meat production is also the position supported by a prominent, but disputed, UN report: *Livestock's Long Shadow* (2006).

However, there may be limits to exactly what this kind of argument shows. It strikes only at intensive farming but not at more traditional forms of animal rearing and thereby does not entail that we should embrace some universal system of vegetarianism or veganism. Moreover, a number of prominent ecologists—J. Baird Callicott and Mark Sagoff in particular—have argued that there is deep rift, and not merely a tension, between consistent ecological concern and a consistent commitment to animal rights. The arguments which they present also seem to generate a level of inconsistency between ecological concern and liberal norms and may therefore be symptomatic of a surprising level of tension between the three adequacy conditions outlined above.

INDUSTRIAL MEAT

Minimally, if we are genuinely concerned about the environment, there does seem to be a good case for adopting either a specialized meat-eating diet or a plant-based (vegetarian or vegan) diet. The case appeals to the built-in, non-eradicable features of industrialized food systems and, in particular, to the fact that industrially produced meat is at least in part (and often for the most part) a form of converted grain and, to a lesser extent, pulses. While cattle are fed on grass to begin with, during the most publicity-friendly stage of the process, for fattening up or 'finishing', they are ordinarily shifted over to a grain-based diet, in sheds or (in the US) in massed feedlots. There, they are given medicated feeds, laced with antibiotics in order to keep any disabling illnesses at bay long enough for the animals to reach slaughter weight. This is the meat that is eaten most of the time in the US and increasingly in Europe also. From the standpoint of the producer, there is a clear rationale for such an approach. It makes their own levels of output independent of the area of land which they, as producers, have at their disposal. Rearing then ceases to be based on the ratio between livestock numbers and the available grassland. From the individual producer's standpoint, it appears more free-floating, no longer so tied to the land.

This, as we might expect, is something of an illusion. There is still an ultimate, indirect but systematic, dependence of meat production on total land area because the grain-feeding system requires that land *somewhere else* is devoted to the farming of feed grains (and, again, pulses). This is not, like *in vitro* meat, a process which is truly land-independent. With an ever-increasing demand for meat in the West, it acts as a driver for forest clearance elsewhere, in areas such as the Amazon where soybeans (a staple livestock feed) are produced, largely for export to the West and especially to the US market. Most of this is, again, not for products such as soya burgers or soy milk, but for animal feed. What makes the process especially odd is that it would be far more efficient for humans to simply source our protein, or at least the component parts of the latter (i.e. amino acids), directly from grains or, more precisely, from various grain–pulse combinations. The conversion of feed into animal body mass is, after all, a notoriously inefficient way for us to source our basic nutrition for the telling reason that most of the nutritional content of what is consumed ends up lost in transition: it is used to support movement, to build bone structure rather than flesh, and lost also through the metabolic inefficiencies of attempting to convert feed into muscle.

On a generous estimate of conversion rates, at the more efficient end of the scale, cows can convert at a rate of somewhere around 1 pound of meat per 13 pounds of grain consumed. Pigs are more efficient, converting at a rate of around 1 pound of meat per 6 pounds consumed. Poultry are superconvertors putting on around 1 pound of body mass per 2–3 pounds of feed. (The latter figure is from Tyson Foods, the largest US producer.) This may give us a clue as to why it is that, after so many millennia of meat-eating, chicken has suddenly become more popular than red meat: fewer of the inputs are lost and so producers and suppliers have a significant vested interest in cultivating a shift of tastes. Yet even with poultry, the overwhelming majority of what is grown for animal feed is not converted into anything which is edible. The process remains intractably wasteful, even to the point where there is regular talk, among the farming community, of a 'farming crisis' brought on by the impracticality of an indefinitely continued extension of the present system.

The attempt to sustain the system also carries a surprisingly high price in terms of energy consumption. The adoption of faster growing crops (such as maize, and especially genetically modified maize) can make a difference, but even such crops are ordinarily dependent on the application of industrial fertilizers. These take a surprising amount of energy to produce because they are based on a mix of nitrogen, potassium and phosphorus, with the nitrogen fixed into the fertilizer through energy-intensive processes of superheating. Most of this energy, indeed most energy of any sort which we have at our disposal, still comes from the burning of fossil fuels, and so, in a sense, we are spreading converted oil and coal onto the fields in order to produce grains and pulses, which will then predominantly be lost to waste, so that a portion will eventually yield meat for the food chain (where, in turn, about a third of what is finally produced will be lost because of dating policy and wasteful non-consumption). This is not, by any obvious standards, ecologically defensible. Nor is it indefinitely sustainable. From an ecological point of view, changes do need to be made. Adopting a plant-based—vegetarian or vegan—diet can allow individual agents to be part of that change.

Quite apart from the cruelty involved in routinely rearing animals on feedlots and inside sheds, away from the daylight, and on anti-biotic-laced grains which evolution has not equipped herbivores to deal with, the system also generates a great deal of low-grade, chemically contaminated waste which cannot be used as fertilizer and which ends up being stored separately until it can be disposed of. In practice, what happens is that the waste seeps into the water system, poisoning rivers and making its way out to sea where (again in the US) it has already polluted extensive stretches of coastal water. The basic flaws of this entire system are not disputed. Indeed, meat producers spend a great deal of time trying to address the more wasteful aspects of the system in order to boost profits while advocates of ethically informed meat-eating appeal to the same set of facts to promote organic, grass-fed and biodynamic farming which cannot yield meat production on any sort of comparable scale. It does seem that only intensive systems can support the levels of meat production which we enjoy in the West and which, elsewhere in the world, are becoming an outward sign of affluence, along with the rising levels of obesity to which the system has also been linked.

The dispute surrounding these matters, and particularly surrounding the *Livestock's Long Shadow* report, centre on exactly *how* damaging the system is, rather than the fact of damage. And, in particular, it focuses on the question of whether meat consumption has now become a greater contributor to global warming than transportation.

The report says 'yes' while critics say 'no' and point to the fact that several of its draftees happen to be vegetarians (although it is not immediately clear that meat-eaters would have been more impartial). The flaws of the system do, however, create at least a prima facie case for dietary change *of some sort*. But while many ecologists and environmentally minded critics are sympathetic to vegetarianism and veganism (with Fearnley-Whittingstall praising the latter for its welcome commitment and ethical consistency) the default position for many ecologists still seems to be one of meat-eating, albeit of a different and ethically informed sort. In part, this is because arguments along the above lines strike only at the industrialized system, and in part it is a matter of concern for the practicalities of turning vegetarianism and veganism into viable universal practices for a population of anything like our current levels. Michael Pollan, in particular, has argued that this *cannot* be done in an ecologically viable manner.

It may, of course, be pointed out that the world's population, especially in the densely populated West, needs to be reduced over the course of time. This is probably true. And a radical population reduction might well make a plant-based system more practical. However, in the meantime, it is tempting to say that 'we are where we are' and that plans must be made which accept that population levels may remain high for some time to come. But even if this did rule out universal vegetarianism or veganism (which is by no means obvious) the adoption of one of the latter diets might still function as a contributory response to a shared predicament.

It has, however, been suggested that while we are entitled to choose our own diet, anything other than a meat-eating diet should not be forced on others, and so vegetarianism (and veganism) should not be forced on children. Instead, they should be reared as meat-eaters until they are old enough to decide matters for themselves. This too is a matter of embracing a broadly liberal set of values with respect for individual choice, and opposition to unnecessary coercion, at their core. But this matters a great deal in terms of the extent to which vegetarianism and veganism could ever contribute to repairing our relations with the rest of the environment, given that extensive dietary change is something which can only take root if it becomes embedded within the food culture and does not have to rely exclusively on some explicit individual choice. The possibility that vegetarianism and/or veganism may become rooted in this way is, however, strongly favoured by a gender imbalance among practitioners. By comparison with countries such as India, where vegetarianism has long been extensive for religious as well as broader cultural reasons, in the West vegetarians and vegans are predominantly (i.e. around three quarters or even four fifths, depending on our preferred surveys) female. And this gender imbalance ensures that the diet has a wider spread across families than might otherwise be the case. Most hetero-sexual female vegetarians do not partner up with male vegetarians because there simply are not enough to go around and so, if and when they do partner up, the question of how couples will eat and how they will raise the children may then become an issue.

What gives this problem of how children ought to be raised a further ecological edge is that environmentalists have long been subject to the charge of authoritarianism and hostility towards liberal norms, partly on the basis that action on climate change would require coercive legislative measures, and partly on the basis that, within a good deal of ecological theory, the interests of the individual are usually required to give way before the interests of the ecosystems in which they are embedded. Environmentalists are, as a result, often sensitive to any perceived clash with core liberal values. If commitment to rearing children on a vegetarian or vegan diet introduces such a clash, this will work strongly against the defensibility of such a diet.

However, it is still not obvious that this consideration alone ought to make the default position for child rearing one of meat-eating. The latter is, after all, just as much a matter of taking decisions *for* children as rearing them on a plant-based diet. What the argument then transposes into is usually a dispute about dietary naturalness or about the idea that humans are naturally meat-eaters or naturally 'omnivores' who have historically combined meat with plant-based foods. But even if this argumentative move is persuasive, it does nonetheless shift the terms of the debate away from any problem of a conflict with liberal norms. Feeding naturally, in these terms, is just as unlikely to involve giving children what they want. What children want, and what many adults also would ideally prefer, is a steady diet of fries, shakes and carbohydrates. At the very least, once an appeal to our standing as omnivores is introduced, the argument against rearing children as anything other than meat-eaters becomes an awkward hybrid of liberal and naturalistic considerations, sitting in tension with each other. And this may be a source of frustration in discussions, as the background norms on which the ethically informed meat-eater draws continually shift around. Yet, at some level, this is perhaps what ethical discussions are always like, and defensibly so, with multiple norms and values in play.

But while there are clear limits to dietary liberalism when it comes to children because, for a large class of dietary issues, they simply cannot be left to choose on their own, there are also some clear limits to a naturalistic appeal because what is natural to humans is precisely dietary *flexibility*. This, we may suspect, is one of the reasons why we are here and why Neanderthal genes form only a fragmentary part of modern human DNA. The Neanderthals, with their heavy meat dependency, have died out and evolution has yielded humans who are capable of surviving on either a meat-free or a meat-inclusive diet. What they (we) are not capable of thriving on are the standard meat-eating diets (especially the Standard American Diet) which would have to qualify as extremely *un*natural. The advocate of vegetarianism and veganism, both of which are (perhaps surprisingly) nutritionally viable for most humans at *all* stages of life, finds they compare favourably to standard diets both in terms of their naturalness and in terms of the choices which they allow to individuals once those individuals reach adulthood. Such choices are not restricted to dietary matters. All other things being equal, healthy adults will have more options than obese adults.

DIETS AND HARM

Yet even if we accept that there is nothing particularly illiberal or unnatural about plant-based diets, there remain several important problems facing the advocate of such diets as *ecologically suitable*. Two, in particular, are striking. Firstly, these diets cannot ordinarily be practised in a way which prioritizes local production; and secondly, insofar as they are dependent on grains, they too require the extensive use of field systems and (as noted in the previous chapter) this carries its own heavy death toll. Indeed, eating grass-fed cattle may be linked to the harm of fewer creatures because of the large number of creatures killed accidentally (yet predictably) as a result of even the most cautious system of harvesting. Automated harvesting kills both directly and predictably, but manual harvesting (although an unlikely anachronism in the West) also leaves a variety of small creatures exposed to predation and without the protective habitats on which they have come to depend.

The lesser of these two problems for the advocate of vegetarianism is the first one. There are various reasons why, from an ecological point of view, it is often a good idea to buy local. Doing so cuts food miles or, more simply, transportation costs and thereby it reduces energy use. It also helps to build a local economy rather than a globalized one which cannot help but be dominated by economic giants whose answerability to liberal democratic structures is compromised. In addition, buying local keeps us more in touch with the origins of our food, which is a way of securing greater transparency within food systems and (more philosophically) a way of *being rooted* in the world.

On such matters, a strange reversal of fortunes occurs, with the vegetarian and vegan able to occupy the standpoint of the pragmatically minded realist. Given current population levels, the idea of a world of local food producers satisfying the demand of local markets seems utterly unrealistic. While there is a reasonable case for promoting local as a counterweight to the unwelcome aspects of globalization, the geographical origin of the food which we consume cannot obviously be more than one consideration among many. It is also a consideration about which we may easily be misled. A great deal of local meat is, on closer examination, transformed Latin American grain. Genuine, comprehensive, grass rearing is rare, although rarer in the US than in Europe. And because grains do not require refrigeration for transportation, the energy costs for their transportation can be low compared with those of local meat production when the latter itself is heavily grain-dependent. On the issue of energy consumption alone, plant-based diets will always tend to fare well, being trumped *only* by meat consumption of a sort which is practically unavailable to the average city-dweller or indeed to anyone who is not themselves connected directly to smallholding. Grains from parts of the world where energy-intensive fertilizers are less heavily used can also trump local meat which is fattened up on grains which are produced through the use of such fertilizers. The vegetarian advocate who wishes to defend the ecological credentials of their dietary practice can plausibly argue that vegetarian frequently, often, and perhaps generally, trumps local.

On the second and more difficult issue—that of the death toll, as a predictable outcome of harvesting—empirical matters also enter into the discussion. It is conceivable that some systems of crop production and harvesting might well yield a large number of creaturely deaths, particularly in the case of animals such as field mice and all manner of smaller creatures, down to the level of insects and worms. It may cause more deaths than the slaughter of a limited number of cattle. The figures for this will not, however, stack up in defence of the existing system of food production—which itself uses crops extensively to feed cattle—but it might well work as a defence of the relatively greater merits of grass-reared cattle. An argument along these lines may to some extent be counterbalanced by the point that the deaths of grain harvesting are unintentional while those involved in animal slaughter are intentional (which *would* make the action much worse). However, there are drawbacks to this claim. Ultimately, it is difficult to envisage a defensible animal ethic which sets aside the basic interests of non-human creatures in favour of the greater importance of human intentions. Moreover, what the lack-of-intention defence appeals to is an application of what is commonly known as the **doctrine of double-effect**: direct harms which are impermissible if intentionally caused, can nonetheless be justified, just so long as they are the unintended (although perhaps predictable) outcome of some action which aims at an important good. The doctrine has, rather notoriously, been appealed to by opponents of abortion in order to defend life-saving operations on pregnant women which, inadvertently but predictably, do result in fetal death.

What makes such a doctrine especially problematic is partly the appearance of being slightly contrived or *only an excuse*, and partly a matter of the disreputable use to which it has been put in defence of various questionable military actions. Here, we might think of the deliberate killing of a number of Israeli civilians, coupled with the killing of a larger number of opposing army personnel, by Palestinian militants in 2014, compared with the inadvertent killing of a vastly larger number of civilians by Israeli bombing whose primary target was combatants, during the same outbreak of violence. Double-effect would seem to justify the latter as ethically more defensible than the former (indeed this was the defence given). And perhaps this would work, on the assumption that civilians genuinely were not being targeted. However, what then has to be taken into account is the *predictable* and perhaps reckless endangerment of civilians together with the sheer and appalling scale of the harm. But if we argue along these lines, that an appeal to double-effect may not excuse extensive harm, we may then be required—as a point of consistency—to argue along the same lines in the case of harvesting. Creatures may not be killed deliberately by the harvesting of grains and pulses, but they are killed *predictably*, and if harvesting can be reduced (by a switch to eating grass-reared cattle) then the many creatures killed during harvesting are perhaps being killed both avoidably and recklessly.

Animal advocates who wish to defend the benefits of plant-based diets not only against the dominant forms of meat-eating, but also against the ecologically informed eating of grass-fed animals, may then have to appeal to the idea that the harm to cattle which results from slaughter, even within ecologically informed systems, is greater than the harm which impacts on a larger number of smaller creatures. Both the approaches of Singer and Regan can make this argument work because they will allow that the harm of death depends on the way in which it frustrates preference satisfaction (and the desires or preferences of the average cow, sheep or pig are likely to be very different from those of any particular field mouse or insect). Any approach towards animal ethics which advocates a more thorough-going species egalitarianism at all levels—from elephants down to beetles—and which accordingly insists that death harms in a uniform manner, may experience difficulties.

ECOLOGICAL CRITICISMS OF ANIMAL RIGHTS

A rather different argument, which seeks to drive a wedge between ecology and rights-based animal advocacy, appeals to the tension between the sheer **individualism** of animal rights and the **holism** and collectivist attitude which is characteristic of ecology. The shared consensus across both approaches is that rights accrue to individuals rather than to collectives. (We may speak about the right of nations to self-determination, but this reduces to the rights of citizens to decide, en masse, whether or not to exercise a certain kind of political autonomy.) An important qualification to this consensus is that at least some eco-theorists do include non-sentient life forms among rights-bearers. On such a view, rights-bearers must still be individuals, and life forms, but they need not be conscious. Trees are the paradigm example. Animal rights supporters, or at least those working within the bounds of moral considerablility which have been fixed by Regan and Singer, tend to hold more restrictively that the individuals in question must be sentient, and that otherwise they simply cannot be candidates for moral standing.

If pressed rigorously (and analytic rigor has been a key aspiration of such accounts) the upshot is that not only trees but forests, streams, mountains and many of the characteristic objects of ecological concern can have neither rights nor interests. Talk about the interests of the planet also has to be figurative, reducible to the interests of sentients or, in Regan's case, perhaps to the interest of a subset of sentient creatures, those who are **subjects-of-a-life**. Advocates of an ecological ethic reject this as **sentientism**. Such a response is typified by those who follow the pioneering Land Ethic set out in Aldo Leopold's *A Sand County Almanac* (1949): whatever promotes the integrity and well-being of the 'biotic community' (i.e. some given ecosystem) is to be supported and whatever fails to do so is to be rejected. This view, which holds considerable influence within ecology, is sometimes known as **Land Ethic holism**. It reverses the order of things which animal rights supporters are used to by favouring the interests of the collective (whatever they may be) over those of the individual. One of the more obvious and disturbing implications of this approach is that if individual animals or groups of animals promote the well-being of the systems which they are part of then they are looked on favourably, but otherwise they are looked on as dispensable or threatening. So, for example, with the removal of predators (such as wolves) various groups of animals (such as deer) have tended to overbreed and may require periodic culling in order to protect the interests of the larger ecosystems of which they form only a replaceable or unnecessary part. For those who accept that this must be done, talk about animal rights, particularly a right not to be killed by humans, may get in the way.

Similarly, we are all aware of the potentially devastating impact of invasive species. Entire ecosystems can become unbalanced as a result. While we may then hope for a new equilibrium to spontaneously emerge, there are some who instead favour 'therapeutic hunting' to protect the ecosystem and, where overpopulation threatens disease, to protect animal populations from their weak and diseased and vulnerable members. (The protective function of this kind of hunting is what is taken to make it therapeutic rather than, for example, recreational.) Animal rights advocates tend not only to reject such claims, but to be suspicious about the sincerity of those who advance them. Arguments for hunting can sometimes be little more than a thinly disguised excuse for blood sports (e.g. for fox hunting or deer stalking in the UK); or little more than scapegoating when industrialized farming has made disease endemic (e.g. culling badgers in the UK in order to tackle bovine tuberculosis); or even an outlet for xenophobia (defending *our* red squirrels against *foreign* grey squirrels, again in the UK). However, at least some prominent ecologists have advanced the case for therapeutic hunting without suggesting that hunting in general fulfils any such role. Here, we may think of Shan Rattenbury, the Green Party minister in the Australian Capital Territory Government who was involved in the promotion of a kangaroo cull in Australia in 2014, apparently as a matter of conviction and much to the dismay of leading figures within his own party.

The upshot of this individualist/collectivist split is that when tensions between environmental ethics and animal rights were first explored during the 1980s, environmental ethics seemed, to animal advocates, promisingly opposed to anthropocentrism, and to human dominance, but insufficiently liberal and protective of the individual creature. The view from the other side of the hill, from environmentalists, was that animal rights approaches (together with Singer's approach) valued the non-sentient too little and the individual creature too much. Faced with the latter criticism, and on the basis that liberal values focus on the individual as a unique, irreplaceable locus of value, Regan labelled strongly holistic and consequentialist versions of environmental ethics, those which did not hesitate to favour culling the weak and the unwanted in order to promote an ideal of systemic health, 'eco-fascism'.

The special target of this charge was J. Baird Callicott, the chief critic of attempts to fuse environmentalism and animal rights. His pivotal article, 'Animal Liberation: A Triangular Affair' (1980), sets out the basic tension between the holism of environmentalists and the individualism of rights theorists. There are three distinctive features of this early Callicott position which are especially worth dwelling on. Firstly, holism based on a conception of the land as a living community; secondly, an exceptionally strict consequentialism;

and finally, an equation of the truly natural with the wild. In line with precisely the kind of anthropocentric mythology which Donna Haraway has challenged, domesticated creatures were regarded as a kind of human artifice. Although the consequentialism echoes Singer, the combination of consequentialism and holism has been staunchly rejected by animal advocates on the ground that, when brought together, they look straightforwardly inconsistent with liberal norms. (Holism on its own is also taken to be objectionable.) The final feature has (perhaps surprisingly) been accepted by many animal rights advocates, and especially those who have come to embrace **extinctionism** in relation to domesticated creatures. Controversial in its own right, this is a move which is likely to undermine the force of any charge of eco-fascism: we would still think badly of the perpetrators of the final solution if it had focused on elimination by group sterilization rather than murder.

A persistent problem for Callicott's early position is that, while appealing to holism, it required either an embracing of authoritarianism—because its attack on rights may equally well be applied to human rights—or else a partitioning of our ethical attitudes between what applies to humans and to non-humans. We may suspect that the latter was, in fact, Aldo Leopold's strong intention: humans can cull non-humans but are not, in turn, candidates for being culled, no matter how numerous we become. Such partitioning can be presented in many forms: individualism for humans and collectivism for animals; liberalism for humans but collectivism for animals; or Kantianism for humans and utilitarianism for animals. Perhaps these options may, on examination, turn out to be one and the same. They do, however, seem to involve a curious form of ethical schizophrenia, a partitioned mode of thinking which is simultaneously a return to anthropocentrism and an abandonment of any plausible claim to ethical holism. The upshot is that environmental ethicists (including Callicott) who remain committed to a thoroughgoing ethical holism have tended to come to the view that, while the charge of eco-fascism was an overstatement, the tension between environmentalism and animal rights was itself also overstated. With this concession made, the disagreement between animal rights and an ecological ethic then begins to look like an 'in-house' quarrel between differently inclined opponents of anthropocentrism. And this may help to explain the continuing and significant overlap between political agents involved in eco-activism and those involved in animal rights activism.

A rather more cautious attempt to drive a wedge between the two was set out by Mark Sagoff in 'Animal Liberation and Environmental Ethics: Bad Marriage, Quick Divorce' (1984), written under the influence of Callicott's early paper, but less willing than the latter to commit explicitly to the environmentalist side. For Sagoff, nature is far worse to most animals than the farmyard. The evolutionary process of natural selection works through the birth of more animals than can survive for even a year. The ways in which a balance is restored, the ways in which they die, and are killed by other animals, are dreadful. If rights are taken to include such basic things as a right to life then we cannot have the smooth functioning of ecosystems *and*, at the same time, a defence of animal rights. Interestingly, Sagoff's conception of what rights involve goes beyond the **negative rights** of Regan and are based around interests, a move which allows him to argue that his critique applies not only to a Regan-style position, which is explicitly framed in terms of rights, but also to a Singer-style position which is framed in terms of interests.

Following David George Ritchie's *Natural Rights* (1916), with its early critique of animal rights, Sagoff argues that, as a matter of consistency, animal rights would have to apply to wild creatures as well as to domesticated animals. In an early application of an argument which has striking similarities to the **argument from marginal cases**, Ritchie argued that whatever natural properties ground the rights of domesticated animals (e.g. properties which generate interests, for example) would also have to ground the rights of wild animals. In his challenge to contemporary animal rights, Sagoff picks up the point and claims that a conception of rights which covers domesticated creatures but does not cover wild animals is not only inconsistent but is sheer sentimentality because it does not extend to where most of the worst animal harms occur. It is blinded by our connection to domesticated creatures and fails to target the place where animal interests are most at stake. While he envisages the possibility of measures to police the wild, the ecological viability of such an approach is questionable. For Sagoff, in the light of this, whatever side of the divide you fall down on, '[e]nvironmentalists cannot be animal liberationists. Animal liberationists cannot be environmentalists.' Joining the two yields a bad marriage and a quick divorce. A good deal of this does, of course, depend on a naturalistic rather than a relational or contractarian grounding for rights. Rights which are based, at least in part, on our relations with animals might encounter no great difficulty in differentiating between the entitlements of different sorts of creatures, such that one group are entitled to protection while another are not. What Sagoff then shows might be the end for a more fine-grained rights theory than a naturalist can give.

A different kind of response to these problems has come from Callicott himself in 'Animal Liberation and Environmental Ethics: Back Together Again' (1988). Rather than being deeply in conflict, Callicott argues that a Leopoldian Land Ethic and an animal rights approach are compatible with one another. However, they do pertain to separate domains. As suggested above, any move of this sort must compromise the holism of the ecological position, but Callicott accomplishes this compromise in a manner which has some strengths. On this revised and compatibilist approach, Mary Midgley was correct to say that pets are part of a mixed community and therefore accrue the entitlements which are due to members of that community. Membership, here, depends on relations of intimacy. On the human side, this involves calling an animal by name, mourning over its death, appreciating its moods, and so on. Such relational connection is a non-arbitrary basis for their moral standing, a standing which may best be understood as a matter of rights. (Effectively, this *is* a relational account of rights.) However, there is no such relational connection in the case of wild animals and the position of the latter is best understood not as members of Midgley's mixed community but as members of Leopold's 'biotic community', without rights and vulnerable to culling or even to therapeutic hunting if this best serves the integrity and condition of the community as a whole.

This marks both a shift in ecological thinking during the 1990s towards more of a compatibilist account of animal rights and ecology. And it also acknowledges special human/animal relations which do seem to warrant special treatment. It does not presuppose that rights must be grounded in the traditional naturalistic manner of Regan. But it yields rights without yielding the range of entitlements which animal advocates and animal rights advocates have characteristically tended to support. John Hadley, from the animal rights side, has pointed out that Callicott's revised view has the alarming consequence of leaving most livestock animals out of the picture, without protection from slaughter. While some may be singled out for special treatment, and bonds of affection may be established, this can hardly be true of most livestock. In the case of laying hens within large sheds, workers barely interact with them on an individual level at all. Accordingly, the relational appeal cannot be the whole story if they too are to be credited with a sufficiently protected standing. The thought here is that even in the absence of any relations with humans there are, surely, some basic moral entitlements, or basic rights, which *any* animal will have, at least insofar as it is an animal which is a candidate for being a rights-bearer at all.

If this is the case, then the position accorded to wild animals by Callicott will still be unacceptable because they too will have at least these same basic rights, and such rights may again, from time to time, conflict with the interests of the biotic community. And perhaps wild animals might have even more entitlements than this. After all, the mixed community is not composed of humans and animals who each have relations of intimacy with one another. Rather, just as with the human community, it is constituted by clusters of individuals who are related to one another in various ways, some of which involve forms of intimacy and care. But such a cluster approach will make it difficult to provide an edge to the mixed community which leaves livestock and wild animals on the outside while, say, leaving a pet dog of a human in some remote area on the inside. Domestic animals befriend other creatures as well as humans, and these creatures in turn befriend still more and other creatures. Callicott's difficulty then will be one which we have encountered before: it is difficult if not impossible to place *all* humans (even hermits, the isolated and the non-communicative) within a single moral community without at the same time lowering the requirements for community membership in ways which may then turn out to be surprisingly inclusive.

CONCLUSION

Animal rights theory may leave us with some tough decisions when it comes to the standing of wild creatures. However, the rights theorist is well placed to argue that the reassuring certainties of certain kinds of environmental ethic are secured only at the expense of blindness to the plight of individual creatures. Relatedly, the tensions between animal rights and liberal norms seem to be less pronounced than initially suspected, less perhaps than those between any strict Land Ethic holism and liberal norms. Indeed, up to a point, animal rights theory can be read as a particular way of articulating liberal norms in light of the fact that humans are embedded in a much larger and predominantly non-human world. Yet the extent to which the recognition of animal rights would be compatible with ecological sustainability remains speculative and the possibility of tensions between environmental concerns and the standing of individual animals remains open. This may be an area in which trade-offs are required.

FURTHER READING

Mark Sagoff, 'Animal Liberation and Environmental Ethics: Bad Marriage, Quick Divorce', *Osgoode Hall Law Journal* 22 (1984): 297–307, presents an often-cited version of the tension between animal rights and environmental ethics and leans on the implausibility of defending animals in the wild. For a classic response to this difficulty, see Stephen L. Clarke's 'The Rights of Wild Things', in an important collection of his essays, *Animals and Their Moral Standing* (London: Routledge, 1997). However, the key text attempting to establish a gulf between animal rights and environmental ethics is J. Baird Callicott, 'Animal Liberation: A Triangular Affair', *Environmental Ethics* 2(4) (1980): 311–38. For the argument that Callicott overstates the tension, see Dale Jamieson, 'Animal Liberation Is an Environmental Ethic', *Environmental Values* 7(1) (1998): 41–57. For Callicott's own rethink, see 'Animal Liberation and Environmental Ethics: Back Together Again' (1988), in Eugene C. Hargrave (ed.), *The Animal Rights/Environmental Ethics Debate* (Albany: SUNY Press, 1992), 249–62. For a critique of Callicott's later position see John Hadley, 'Critique of Callicott's Biosocial Moral Theory', *Ethics & the Environment* 12(1) (2007): 67–78.

The UN report on the impact of meat-eating, *Livestock's Long Shadow: Environmental Issues and Options* (Rome: Food and Agriculture Organization of the United Nations, 2006), can be accessed online at the *FAO Corporate Document Repository*, <http://www.fao.org/docrep/010/a0701e/a0701e00.htm> (accessed 14 October 2014).

THE POLITICAL TURN

Accounts of animal ethics have tended to focus heavily on giving reasons to restrict or eliminate the harms that humans do. In terms of rights theory, this has generated a tendency to focus on **negative rights** rather than **positive rights**. The contrast here is between freedoms from harm and various positive entitlements, entitlements to be supported or enabled rather than merely left alone. **Extinctionism** feeds on this tendency: those animals who cannot be left to their own devices are to be bred out of existence, leaving only the free and the wild (in the sense of those creatures who are *both* free and wild). In light of the extent and character of the harms which animals have suffered at the hands of humans, this focus on negative rights, on *being left alone*, is understandable. However, such a negative or non-interventionist focus may fail to provide a plausible picture of how things might, overall, be different. That is to say, it will fail to provide a plausible account of 'the endgame' of animal ethics or, in familiar activist terms, a plausible account of what **animal liberation** might actually look like, in the absence of some manner of apartheid in which humans and non-humans are left to occupy radically distinct spaces.

And here, the request for more of a story about the endgame of animal liberation need not involve a quest for some wildly conjectural account of utopia. Rather, it may be understood as the request for some rudimentary account of the kind of standing (legal, ethical, political) that animals might actually acquire as they continue to live with and alongside us. In recent years, discussions of animal ethics (at least in the analytically influenced tradition of Singer and Regan) have increasingly been concerned with the political dimensions of such standing. There has been what is sometimes referred to as a **political turn**, although there is no single agreed definition of what this turn involves or whether the very idea of such a turn is a good way of representing matters. The arguments for animal rights and for animal liberation have, after all, had a strongly political dimension from the outset, and the main theories have always been shaped by key liberal values, particularly through a commitment to some form of equality (but not necessarily a commitment to **strong species egalitarianism**). A political dimension to the discussion is not, therefore, something new. It has always been there.

In addition, the texts which have helped to give rise to the idea of a turn have also differed from one another in significant ways. They have not established any single new paradigm to replace the older Singer–Regan one or Gary Francione's **abolitionist** challenge to the latter. And this too may lead us to wonder about the sense in which there is a cohesive challenge to an older orthodoxy. Even so, there does seem to be at least some case for stressing the shift into a more political register. But while politicizing texts by Robert Garner, Alastair Cochrane, Will Kymlicka and Sue Donaldson as well as Siobhan O'Sullivan may not outline a shared paradigm, when taken together they do nonetheless contain a number of overlapping commitments which serve to highlight the political dimensions of animal ethics. The following in particular seem noteworthy although perhaps no one theory subscribes to them all:

1 A clearer focus on the tension between the treatment of animals and core liberal values.

2 The return to a strong emphasis on animal interests but in the context of a rights theory rather than a Singer-style consequentialism.

3 An emphasis on positive rights rather than negative rights or welfare considerations alone.

4 A downgrading of the argument from marginal cases so that it is called on only to play a localized (rather than central) role.

5   Consideration of animal interests *as part of the* **common good**.
6   A conception of the animal rights movement as *primarily* a political movement rather than a moral crusade.
7   A broadly pragmatic attitude towards political engagement and compromise, an attitude which contrasts strongly with abolitionism (at least insofar as the latter is articulated by Francione).

These are recurring themes of some of the most innovative and influential contemporary work on animal ethics. Taken together, they are indicative of just how far matters have moved on from the dominant first-wave accounts of animal rights and liberation even if they have not yet coalesced into a new orthodoxy.

DRAWING ON LIBERAL NORMS

Liberal norms have always been closely connected with our modern conception of democracy. Indeed, there is a case for regarding democracy not simply as a set of procedures (various sorts of electoral systems, universal suffrage, and so on) but rather as an expression of liberal values. And so, where we do not have the combination of the two, the liberal and the democratic, we ordinarily hold that something has gone wrong.

The most important liberal norms of all, at least on most contemporary articulations of liberalism, are those concerning equality, individual freedom (liberty and tolerance), and the avoidance of cruelty (we do not take revenge on enemies and violence is to be kept to a minimum rather than admired). The inclusion of the latter may seem striking, given that it has no counterpart in the classical triumvirate of liberty, equality and fraternity. However, Richard Rorty and Judith Shklar have independently suggested that liberalism involves *putting cruelty first* as the most grievous of all failings, thereby allowing it to displace the classic Christian identification of pride as the fault which grounds all others. Liberalism, by effecting this pride-to-cruelty shift, dovetails well with the idea that the public domain should be shaped in a broadly secular manner.

But while the rejection of cruelty has come to be increasingly central to our contemporary idea of a liberal society and to our understanding of appropriate agency, commitment to the importance of fraternity has somewhat waned. And this may be problematic.

Jacques Derrida, among others, has suggested that the result is an impoverished conception of politics, one which threatens to undermine any sense of solidarity amongst members of the political community. This inclusive approach contrasts with an important, decades-long trend within analytic political philosophy. The latter has tended to emphasize, perhaps overemphasize, the separateness of liberalism and communitarianism. This is something we have already encountered, for example in the attempts to set (individualist) animal rights and (collectivist) ecology against one another. And no doubt there are significant distinctions which may be drawn, but they may also be drawn rather too sharply. Any rigid dichotomy between liberalism and communitarianism may make the idea of the liberal community difficult to situate. And this will be awkward given that many of us aspire to live in, and be part of, communities of just this sort.

A more localized symptom of the displacing of fraternity from the core norms of liberalism is the way in which the idea of community (whether that of a mixed community or of a human community) has been so difficult to situate within otherwise liberal approaches towards the standing of animals. Singer and Regan both take the individual creature to be the basic unit of analysis and then, presupposing a sharp individual/community distinction, they find difficulty accommodating more communitarian-minded talk about **our common humanity**. The latter then seems like a communitarian myth or **speciesism**, pure and simple, while to those like Cora Diamond and Raimond Gaita, the importance of this shared humanity should be obvious, something which we can only overlook or set aside if we are in the grip of a theory.

A major difficulty for contemporary animal ethics is figuring out a way to incorporate insights of the latter sort (if indeed they are insights) while retaining a sense of the importance of an appeal to liberal norms which may then help to underpin the standing of animals as unique, individual creatures who are not there simply for our use and convenience. However, any move of the latter sort will depend on convincing those with a more anthropocentric conception of the world that liberal norms extend all the way out, or at least they extend much further than nineteenth-century liberals imagined: they do not just govern our relations with other humans but concern a way of responding to all sorts of creatures.

While many of us do subscribe to a broadly liberal outlook on the world, such a liberal attitude is partially suspended where animals are concerned, it is narrowed down to the avoidance of cruelty, thought of as gratuitous or unnecessary harm. Ideas of equality and liberty are then taken to apply more strictly to humans. And it is precisely this restriction which Singer and Regan sought to challenge. Few, if any, of the harms which we endorse and inflict on animals could be sanctioned if we were ever to commit to the idea that animals are our moral equals and deserving of freedom from domination. And so we may identify a tension between a thoroughgoing liberalism and a more restricted liberalism which seeks to live in a world which is partitioned into the human and the non-human.

Political-turn texts incline towards the former, towards a more thoroughgoing liberalism. Siobhan O'Sullivan's *Animals, Equality and Democracy* (2011) is a case in point. O'Sullivan argues that, as a matter of equality, the standing of all animals ought to be in line with the standing which we accord to the best-treated animals. Failure to adopt this approach is taken to involve inconsistency or, more simply, favouritism and bias. O'Sullivan's approach shares a strongly Kantian influence with Singer and Regan in the sense that it involves an appeal to impartial standards, an appeal to a sense that the same rules should apply to all. However, she accepts the politically problematic nature of applying this in a way which requires a commitment to strong species egalitarianism. And so, instead of pressing for the recognition of an inconsistency in our treatment of non-humans by comparison with humans (the 'external inconsistency') she presses for recognition of another inconsistency, one which exists between our treatment of different sorts of animals (the 'internal inconsistency').

This involves a shift in attention which is, in part, a strategic move. Focusing on the external inconsistency, in the Singer, Regan and Francione manner—by appeal to the argument from marginal cases—has turned out to be politically ineffective, or effective only up to a point. It has not fundamentally shifted attitudes or fed through into appropriate legislative protection for non-humans. As an acceptance of political realities, a redirecting of the **animal advocate**'s case is therefore required. In line with this, O'Sullivan draws attention to the unreasonable way in which we discriminate between one and another non-human species and between one and another member of the same species. If, for example, we were asked why we treat dogs in ways which utterly exclude the very idea that they might be consumed, we will in all likelihood identify properties (intelligence, sociability, affectionate nature, and so on) which are also properties of pigs (and perhaps some other livestock animals also) which are nonetheless subject to slaughter. Our assumption that a plausible reason for differential treatment can be given will not stand up to scrutiny. This does not involve an appeal to the argument from marginal cases, but it does involve a similarly *comparative* approach.

It could, no doubt, be argued that in the case of certain species there is a permission-granting historic dimension to such bias; however, this argument will not be available in cases where the differently treated animals belong to exactly the same species. Here, we may think of the lives of agricultural animals by comparison with those of companion animals. A horse may be one or the other, and this fact alone will make a great deal of difference to its quality of life and to the harms which it may face. Yet this difference is not always grounded in biology or in the respective properties of the creatures concerned. Nor is it grounded in the historical connections which we have with one species but not with another.

What O'Sullivan highlights here is precisely the kind of inconsistency which Cora Diamond has long been suggesting that animal advocacy should appeal to rather than placing so much weight on the argument from marginal cases. Inconsistency of this sort is also something which ordinary, non-partisan agents *are* typically sensitive to. It does seem unfair that one animal should be treated kindly (on a certain understanding of kindness) while another of exactly the same type should be made to suffer dreadfully.

In defence of such differential treatment, supporters of animal use often point to the demands of economics. The treatment of animals, like the treatment of humans, is often a function of their economic role. And this is not likely to change anytime soon. A racehorse will, for example, be treated very differently from a working horse; a hen in someone's backyard, very differently from one in an industrial-scale laying shed. And so the relational position of animals enters into the picture of just what they are entitled to, just as it does, in practice, with humans. But this can seem to imply that economically driven inequalities trump the idea of equality before the law, a claim which some Marxists might agree with as a brute fact about capitalism, but such a view is hardly available to a supporter of liberal democracy. If we are serious about equality before the law, economic imperatives cannot, or cannot always, be trumps.

It is also worth reflecting on the fact that an appeal to economic realities does not seem to do enough work to explain our actual tolerance of animal harms. Anyone who kept a group of hens open to public view and under industrial farming conditions would quickly find themselves in trouble even if they were able to point towards economic pressures or the prevailing market conditions. Acquiescence in the face of animal harms relies not only on an acceptance of economic rationale—it also depends on such harms being kept away from view. For O'Sullivan, our readiness to discriminate between animals, and accept poorer standards for many, is based on keeping them out of sight, away from the eyes of the political community. Here, we might think of the shock that holidaymakers from the US, UK and Australia experience when they see finches, canaries and parrots confined together in small cages. To many, this may seem dreadful and aberrant. Yet these conditions are the norm in the domestic egg and poultry production systems of their home countries. The factor guiding acquiescence, according to O'Sullivan, is the keeping of harms away from democratic scrutiny.

This is an important argumentative move. Concealment runs counter to an ideal of openness which has gone hand in hand with democracy from its very beginnings. (The founding statement of democracy, Pericles' *Oration*, set down in antiquity, explicitly connects democracy with such openness.) Continuation of the state of affairs in which any animals are subject to such harms is, therefore, based on a lack of effective community access to knowledge about what goes on. This makes impartiality, in line with the best current standards of treatment, not simply a matter of applying a precautionary principle to avoid cruelty. Rather, it makes an impartial application of the best standards democratic because only such standards have emerged out of open public awareness and informed debate. The standards governing concealed mistreatment have been fixed, instead, by some or other private agency or by some or other financial or political elite. The upshot then is that the inconsistency in our treatment of animals is based on a violation of the political community's right to decide. Effectively, O'Sullivan's case is an appeal to the popular will.

This is also an approach which avoids the dangers of what we might call 'frictionless theory', i.e. theory which is produced without reference to or influence from actual patterns of political engagement. In O'Sullivan's case, her approach has been directly shaped by political activism of a sort pioneered in Australia. The 1970s and 1980s saw the emergence of the Animal Liberation Front (ALF) in the US and the UK, in parallel with the first wave of animal rights and liberation literature. The ALF covertly rescued animals from laboratories and adopted a paramilitary iconography with balaclavas, combat clothing and animals held across the chest like assault rifles. The imagery is both misleading (given that the ALF defends violence against property but not against persons) and arguably it is unsuited to the political climate in which we now live, in the aftermath of the terrorist attacks of 9/11. In the 1990s, in an attempt to shift animal rights activism away from this unhelpful public image, activists associated with organizations such as Animal Rights Victoria pioneered **open rescue**, a practice shaped by Gandhian principles of civility and non-violence. Animals are rescued from situations of extreme harm, well in excess of anything which the public will tolerate, and the plight of these animals and the identity of rescuers is then made open to public scrutiny.

This is an approach which has received a good deal of media sympathy and public support. But it has not, in fact, displaced ALF activities. Open rescue is directed at the food system but its openness is problematic in the case of lab animals partly because such openness could make rescued but valuable animals, those animals who constitute an investment of time and work, too easy to recover. In the case of rescue from food production systems, the owners do not tend to want recovery because individual animals have little commercial value and their reintroduction might, in any case, constitute a biohazard, a danger of contamination. Even so, open rescue has been well received internationally, and is now practised in Europe and the US, albeit with variations on the initial model and with varying levels of success. The crux of the matter, however, has been the emphasis on letting the public see and decide. And while this strategy may now have run its course in the Australian heartlands, with court costs and time demands slowly taking their toll on the organizations and individuals concerned, O'Sullivan's position is, in part, a legacy of its open and democratic ethos, a legacy which is likely to shape future patterns of activism at an international level, as animal rights activists seek to leave behind the imagery of the ALF and, with it, vulnerability to the charge that they are akin to some manner of domestic terrorists.

DIFFERENCE VERSUS UNIFORMITY

O'Sullivan appeals to impartiality in the face of bias, the bias represented by the 'internal inconsistency'. But, as with Singer's approach, there is a concern that inconsistency in our responses might be removed by levelling-down rather than levelling-up. What if a principle of equal treatment was adopted, as a result of robust public deliberation, with open scrutiny of the matter in hand, and it was then decided that, for economic reasons, *all* animals should be treated in line with the weakest of constraints? O'Sullivan seems ready to bite this particular bullet—at least in theory, and in the interests of liberal values—albeit on the understanding that such a scenario would never actually arise. This is not accidental, the only standards likely to secure informed public support *are* the higher standards, in part because lesser standards will clearly violate the liberal commitment to avoid cruelty and, in part, because agents will always be unwilling to regard their companion animals, creatures whom they love, as fair game for lower-standard mistreatment.

Because of this, endorsement of anything short of the highest standards would never happen as the result of any *genuinely* open process of democratic deliberation by actual agents. The latter are very different from agents who deliberate behind a **veil of ignorance**, and with their bonds to others bracketed out of consideration. In practice, lower standards of animal treatment do seem to depend on concealment and misrepresentation, albeit misrepresentation in which the private citizen is somewhat implicated by looking the other way. (The point about deliberate evasion, which we encountered in the discussion of the controversial Holocaust analogy in Chapter 6, applies.) Even so, we might still wonder about the level of commitment to liberal political norms which makes levelling-down seem even theoretically permissible, if unlikely. It may seem that our rights, as members of the political community—to disclosure and choice—have been allowed more importance than the interests of animals themselves. However, we might do well to bear in mind that O'Sullivan's approach results not from any deep level of value metaphysics but rather from a pragmatic and strategic approach which involves beginning from agreed liberal norms in order to reach an animal-favouring agreement. This is a strategy which carries risks, most especially because liberal norms are so often articulated in anthropocentric terms. Yet it may be a strategy which could be more politically effective than falling back on either form of species egalitarianism in combination with an appeal to the argument from marginal cases.

A rather different, and perhaps more forceful, objection is that O'Sullivan's approach makes precisely the kind of homogenizing move which Derrida identifies as part of the package which legitimizes our mistreatment of others (and not just animal others). When a sense of particularity is lost or simply set aside, the standing of the unique individual is unavoidably compromised. O'Sullivan does cluster together very different sorts of individual creatures into the one large non-human bundle. A further pragmatic consideration may, however, do some work here. We may have to accept that such clustering is going to happen (it already does) and that animal advocates have to work with it. But perhaps a more conciliatory response can also be given. Perhaps our very different relations to different sorts of creatures can be used to rationalize and justify different forms of treatment. Relational approaches towards animal ethics may be correct about that point. Yet it would be odd to adopt a standpoint which was relational through and through, which did not accept that there is a minimal baseline of acceptable treatment irrespective of how we as individuals are connected to the animals in question.

A liberal attitude, with a built-in requirement that we avoid cruelty, does just this. It applies irrespective of how we are connected to other creatures. However, the endorsement of a baseline of defensible treatment comes at a price. Actions carried out within the experimental system, and which are deemed 'necessary' to research, are often deemed to be permissible rather than cruel even though, were they to occur in other contexts, their cruelty would be obvious. Baseline constraints tend to come with special exceptions which may seem to be justified because the constraints act as a reassurance that matters are generally well handled. And, quite apart from this, any baseline constraints which are thought through in

O'Sullivan's terms (by levelling up the constraints to that of our best practices) will be far more demanding than the simple exclusion of cruelty alone, and so a sense of controversy returns.

Even so, some level of clustering of animals together for the sake of legislative protection may be unavoidable if they are to have any protection at all. In our personal lives, we may encounter companion animals (like Derrida's little cat, mentioned in the opening chapter) as individual creatures. But the very nature of public policy and the political is that it is more general, even though this risks the possibility that our individuality and that of others may sometimes be lost sight of. But while O'Sullivan favours uniform standards for the treatment of animals, Donaldson and Kymlicka's *Zoopolis: A Political Theory of Animal Rights* (2011) argues that clustering need not be the same as adopting a single big response to the plight of animals. Instead, they suggest that domesticated animals should be regarded as part of our political community, wild animals should be regarded as part of sovereign communities (which we are not part of) and 'liminal' animals who cross boundaries should be seen as visitors or resident outsiders in our midst.

While it has still been charged with clustering too many types of differing creatures together, this approach does mark an important move away from the ethos of negative rights. None of the identified groups (animal citizens, liminal animals and sovereign communities of wild animals) are to be regarded as others who should simply be left alone. We all live in one and the same world. Animal citizens are creatures who, through human agency, have been brought into our society and rendered dependent on it. This applies not only to companion animals but to domesticated animals more generally, not just pets but livestock also. And because we have brought them into our society in a dependent condition, we have obligations towards them as beings who are part of our mixed community. The traditional way of recognizing such standing is through the extending of citizenship rights. What this involves is not simply rights of residency and return, and not simply (as in Singer and as is the case with current legislative protection) an entitlement to have their interests considered. Rather, it involves having their interests considered as part of the common good.

Wild animals, by contrast, or 'truly wild' animals—i.e. creatures with their own territories who generally shun contact with humans—do not form a community with us. This underpins what Claire Palmer has called the 'laissez-faire intuition' that, unlike domesticated creatures, they should be left to their own devices. They may nonetheless form communities with each other, communities which may have reasonable territorial claims made on their behalf. They may have entitlements to compensatory measures for various sorts of legitimate and non-legitimate incursions into their territory. But this is not a case for geographical apartheid. Rather, in their own territory, we are the visitors and they are the citizens, we must accommodate ourselves to them.

Finally, there are creatures who live in our midst but independently so, indeed we and they may have little direct interaction. Mice would be an obvious example, urban foxes would be another. By recognizing these animals as a distinct and significant group, Donaldson and Kymlicka help to break apart the long-standing domesticated/wild binary dichotomy, and with it they pose a significant problem for extinctionism. There is a class of animals who cannot readily be bred out of existence. That would have been done already if it was at all possible. Yet they are subject to relations of dependency with humans. Many live on what we leave behind. Such creatures are denizens, resident aliens. The rights which are most relevant to their interests concern tolerant coexistence. But, because we cannot help but to impact on their lives, these rights must stretch beyond the negative entitlement to be left alone. Should we destroy habitat (as human activity regularly does) we may be duty-bound to provide them with alternative options.

This is an elegant but, for some, rather utopian way of making sense of how animals might be included explicitly within the domain of the political, governed as it is by liberal norms. It has given rise to three key objections. Firstly, this would be citizenship without proper political agency. It would not be real citizenship at all for the simple reason that animals cannot take on the responsibilities and duties which go with citizenship. Perhaps negative rights need not belong to those who also have duties but the positive rights of citizenship seem to do so. Yet here we may provide a response which echoes the argument from marginal cases: there are humans in a similar predicament, humans who cannot exercise familiar forms of political agency. Instead, advocacy and enabled agency are required. But this is simply part and parcel of belonging to a genuinely inclusive political community. The objection reverts to the flawed idea that we face the world as individuals and not as the socially embedded beings that we are. While negative rights are thoroughly consistent with a strict individualism, positive rights require a social context. And this applies with humans just as much as it applies in the case of non-humans.

Secondly, it may be charged (and has been charged) that animal citizenship, however modified, would be excessively demanding. An ecological variant of this is that regarding wild animals as citizens of sovereign animal communities, rather than members of biotic communities, would be disastrous. Culling by outsiders (ourselves) for the sake of system health would be difficult to justify. One of the more comforting responses here involves accepting a blanket ban on any such intervention. This may not be as impractical a move as it might seem. Systems do, ultimately, tend to reach their own equilibrium, albeit under altered conditions. And it is certainly problematic to imagine that it is our responsibility to impose a stasis on the natural world through the indefinite preservation of all endangered species.

However, systems collapse as well as change, and they may pose a threat to their neighbours. Our responsibilities then would be a variation on those we acknowledge in the case of other human communities, up to and including intervention. An impending crisis may require a humanitarian response. A difficulty, in practice, is that such responses are generally used to introduce and bolster patterns of domination. But this is a problem of an utterly familiar sort and does not identify any unique difficulty with the recognition of sovereign animal communities. More generally, the Donaldson and Kymlicka approach would demand all sorts of changes in human/ animal relations. Most obviously, we would have to stop using animals as food. But objections which suggest not just the demands of this approach, but its *excessive* demandingness, tend to identify problems which already exist with regard to respecting a full range of human rights. Such objections do not identify anything which is radically new, but simply the difficulties of sticking by a consistent commitment to liberal democracy rather than suspending the latter periodically and locally as a matter of convenience.

Finally, a familiar objection is that many of the individual animal entitlements which Donaldson and Kymlicka argue for may be defensible, but marketing this as a form of citizenship is politically impractical. It clashes dreadfully with a sense of realpolitik, a sense that citizenship pertains exclusively to human relations. This objection is open to a charge of speciesism, but here we may be inclined to accept that *ought* implies *can*, that to say 'things ought to be different' is to imply that they could be different. And the whole point, in the present case, is that this may not be so. There may simply be a limit to which humans are capable of acknowledging other creatures as, in some qualified sense, our equals. In the attempt to remove species prejudice we may find ourselves pressed up against the limits of human moral psychology, against restrictions which are neither chosen nor capable of being removed while we remain the creatures that therefore we are.

Even a consistent **weak species egalitarianism** may be out of reach. By contrast, a strong species egalitarianism may simply be unlivable, or possible only as a statistical exception, out on the further edges of our variable human behaviour. And while we may speculate about the future, and about what may succeed our kind of human, a pragmatic acceptance that we cannot have all that we might wish for must surely be built into any workable liberalism. This may mean that citizenship, a concept which is full of historical significance, may be privileged, set apart from our attempts to include animals within a politicized conception of fellow creatures. Matters here remain speculative. An appeal to realpolitik suggests just such an exclusion, but a genealogical account of the concept of citizenship could show that it has always been more malleable than we might imagine, and so a further leap across the species boundary might be possible. Moreover, beneath the apparent utopianism of Donaldson and Kymlicka's approach we might find a tough-minded realism about exactly how much our political arrangements have to change.

PRAGMATISM AND JUSTICE

A crucial respect in which Donaldson and Kymlicka's approach differs from other key political-turn texts is in the extent to which a future which differs from the present is envisaged. O'Sullivan's approach is more pragmatic, more strategic—and in this respect, more typical. Faced with an apparently intractable refusal of humans to regard other creatures as our equals, she focuses on the idea that we might nonetheless regard them as equal to each other, and that this might yield a major step forward in standing for most animals. This pragmatism, the sense that arguments need to connect up with where people actually are, has been the driving force behind most of the core political-turn texts. This inclination towards pragmatism is, in part, a response to the impact of abolitionism in the US and to the perception of the latter as puritanical, or fundamentalist or at least incapable of reaching out towards political opponents. Many of the most important political-turn texts have come from the UK and Australia, where the conditions which gave rise to US abolitionism, and its cultural motifs (rebranding animal rights as analogous to the movement against slavery), have less sway.

Pragmatism in this context has fed through in a dual manner. On the one hand, it has fed through into the view that an effective animal rights activism will have to be (i) compliant with liberal political norms, under which the law may sometimes be broken, but only in certain ways; and (ii) part of a cohesive political movement rather than a personal moral crusade which prioritizes lifestyle over impact. Open rescue, of the sort which has influenced O'Sullivan's work, serves as an exemplar of liberally informed lawbreaking. Lobbying for legislative change serves as an exemplar of moving beyond lifestyle choices and into the terrain where only a political movement can be effective. An emphasis on the need for such a shift can be found in the writings of long-standing animal rights activist Kim Stallwood. Yet the complex ties between lifestyle choice and animal rights activism ensure that both have a political significance. An emphasis on spreading lifestyle-based veganism and vegetarianism continues to be regarded as important but is not given the primacy that vegan outreach has for a Francione-style abolitionist.

On the other hand, at the level of political theory, the shift towards pragmatism has fed through into the view that a political theory of animal rights will have to include both a conception of ultimate goals (an ideal theory) and a strong non-ideal component. The most systematic account of this ideal/non-ideal combination is set out in Robert Garner's *A Theory of Justice for Animals* (2013), the pragmatic overtones of which should be clear from the outset. While we may find it difficult to situate the idea of animal citizenship, there is little dispute about the idea that our relations with animals ought to be governed by a sense of justice. (The Rawlsian exclusion of animals from the domain of justice, outlined in Chapter 4, is an exception to the norm.) The thought behind the contrast between ideal and non-ideal theory is that normative claims, such as animal rights claims, should not run too far ahead of what can be politically accepted. Ideal theory should spell out what John Rawls refers to as a realistic utopia, i.e. a state of affairs which is consistent with what we know about human nature. It should not be an actual, full-blooded utopia—a state of affairs too demanding for humans. Non-ideal theory, by contrast, starts from where we are, from the historically given and culturally constrained circumstances under which we happen to live. A valid non-ideal theory will nonetheless support normative claims which are *consistent with* the pursuit of the more ideal situation. And it is this commitment to a connection between the two which makes it difficult to regard this approach as mere welfare advocacy, by contrast with a genuine animal rights position.

This meta-attitude towards political theory shapes Garner's response to the three key questions: (1) Can animals be worthy recipients of justice? (2) What do animals gain from being recipients of justice? and (3) What are animals due as a matter of justice? His answer to the first question is a resounding 'yes'. Attempts to exclude animals from the domain of justice, to effectively situate them outside of the bounds of entitlement to political consideration, do not withstand careful scrutiny. The best-known case for doing so—Rawlsian exclusion on the basis that animals cannot be parties to a contract—is deemed to have generated too many inclusion problems. Cognitively impaired humans and future generations require ad hoc theoretic adjustment, or else they lose their entitlements. Garner's answer to the second question centres on the point that justice is the standard political currency of our times; it frames matters in terms which call for legislative support by the state. Talk about the virtues, or attenuated (more ethical than political) talk about rights *alone*, misses the crucial nexus between justice and the enactment of law (also its enforcement). Accordingly, claims about justice should be the preferred discourse of animal advocates as a way of simultaneously improving the lot of animals and moving towards an ideal state of affairs. However, this may remain somewhat vague without a response to the third question, a specification of what animals are actually due as a matter of justice.

What they are due turns out to be rights. Welfare consideration alone does not yield enough as a response to animal interests. And it is notable that, here, Garner presses an interest-based account of rights rather than a more Kantian autonomy or **subjects-of-a-life** account. Rights are based on the possession of strong interests. Precedents for this move include the rights theorists Joseph Raz and Joel Feinberg; and the move, when made in the context of animal ethics, does help to overcome the long-standing division generated by the Singer/Regan dispute about whether interests or rights are the proper focus of animal ethics. It also gives content to the suspicion that, over a large range of issues, Singer and Regan are deploying different but equivalent vocabularies. However, interest-basing along the lines that Garner proposes also leads to a rejection of strong species egalitarianism. While suffering seems *equally* to run contrary to the interests of humans and non-humans, the continuation of life and the securing of liberty do not obviously do so. We can readily appreciate why this might be the case for reasons already explored. Ending the life of an animal is typically contrary to its interest, but animals do not typically form complex desires about the future, desires whose satisfaction is contingent on their own future survival. Similarly, animals do not seem to require the same kinds of autonomy as humans in order to flourish, they do not shape their self-esteem in terms of conceptions of freedom and liberty. And so, when it comes to life, liberty and the pursuit of happiness, animal interests and human interests are not to be understood in exactly the same manner. Moreover, for Garner, recognition of this difference is deeply embedded in cultural attitudes towards the non-human in a way which simply *cannot* be uprooted. Given this, a strong species egalitarian version of animal rights will fail to meet the Rawlsian test for a valid ideal theory. It will not be consistent with a realistic utopia.

Instead of species egalitarianism, Garner opts for the 'enhanced sentience position' as his ideal theory: animals have a right not to have suffering inflicted on them, not even as a trade-off for familiar consequentialist gains, but they do not have a right to life or to liberty. This is (in obvious respects) controversial. As a point of clarification, he is not arguing for the position which Alasdair Cochrane has recently advanced, using a similarly interest-basing approach: the view that animals simply lack *any* intrinsic interest in liberty. Instead, Garner is claiming that although animals *do* have interests in both liberty and life, interests which should be given their due, these interests are insufficiently strong to ground a right. As an ideal theory this will probably meet the Rawlsian requirements for advocacy of a realistic utopia. However, it does set a goal which many animal advocates will regard as insufficiently constraining on human action. Challenges may be anticipated by appeal to a revised conception of the harms of death and the ways on which they impact on animals.

The constraints on human action are loosened even further by Garner's non-ideal theory, the 'sentience position', which prohibits the inflicting of suffering on animals by humans but accepts certain forms of animal use which include the sacrificing of animal lives for human benefit. Such use clearly does involve harm, but a violation of animal rights only if it also involves the inflicting of suffering (and not only death). This constraint would still be strong enough to require us to close down industrial meat production and most of the experimental system, together with various allied practices, but it would not exclude all slaughter for consumption or all forms of experimentation. It would not give those who regard themselves as abolitionists, in Francione's sense, what they want. Yet it would require a change which, if offered, most animal advocates might seize eagerly and with both hands. Indeed, it would be odd not to endorse such a change unless we happened to believe on a priori grounds that no concession short of the ideal can ever contribute to the realizing of it. If we share Garner's pragmatic intuitions, we may then look sympathetically on his claims if critically on some of the detail.

This does, however, make the areas in which Garner is liable to be attacked fairly clear: neither the ideal nor the non-ideal theory comprehensively displaces everything that might be regarded as anthropocentrism or speciesism. It does not set out a version of animal liberation, because animals are deemed to have no deep interest in, hence no right to, liberty. But the problem here may belong with those who wish to retain an idea of animal liberation, given that the latter is often understood in terms which are either implausible (e.g. a simplifying extinction of all domesticated creatures which thereby excludes further rights violations) or else badly conceived (supporters of liberation want something, not *this*, not what we have now—but they are not sure what). Nonetheless, the severance of animal rights from animal liberation does itself remain contingent on a particular, questionable conception of the latter. The content of what animal liberation would have to involve is presupposed to be close to what abolitionists have called for. This would require an end to the property status of animals and an end to all forms of animal use. Liberation, thus understood, might well involve extinctionism. Yet if this is liberation then it goes far beyond anything which has resulted from the end of human slavery in the US or the end of the feudal system in Europe. Neither of the latter involved a comprehensive end to the use of the liberated. Rather, the liberated were subject to altered forms of control and dependence. On a revised and more modest conception of animal liberation, the kind which one might expect a political pragmatist to advance, it might turn out to be something in which animals do have a deep or strong interest. In which case they would also, by Garner's own criteria, have a right to it.

On the straightforward plus side, Garner's non-ideal theory does look normatively much closer than previous approaches to a strengthened version of the position on animal treatment which is advocated by many eco-activists and -theorists. The preferred terminology—of justice first and rights as an aspect of justice—is also less embedded in the kind of individualism which has been a source of regular ecological concern. As such, it reinforces the view that the divisions between animal rights and ecological concerns have been over-stated. And this in turn promotes the kind of activist rapprochement which may be required in order to build an effective political constituency, even if Garner's ideal theory does then go on to make Rawlsian concessions to ineradicable anthropocentrism: even the ideal may seem to accept a sense of human superiority *in some respects*. Yet, while Garner assumes that this requires an abandonment of the terrain of species egalitarianism, what is meant by the latter may look suspiciously close to strong species egalitarianism. It is less obvious that this approach must conflict with weak species egalitarianism. Consistency with the latter might provide at least some defence against the charge that too many concessions are made to speciesism, and too little vision shown about just how different the future might be.

A final and rather different line of criticism touches on the concern with which this text opened: the division between unifying and relational theories. A heavy dose of pragmatism may be just what animal ethics needs, especially in the aftermath of the strongly utopian component of the tradition which began with Singer and

Regan and which gathered strength in the writings of Gary Francione. But there is a dimension of the Regan/Singer legacy to which Garner may perhaps remain a little too faithful: their commitment to the view that one big idea, such as consequences, or interests or rights, should be appealed to in order to do most of the work. But while justice may do more and better work than the previous candidates, it is not obvious that such a heavy focus on any single concept is our only or best option. Indeed, if we are in the business of pragmatically tracking how humans actually deliberate about ethics then some form of normative pluralism may be preferable. Indeed, pragmatism and normative pluralism may seem like natural bedfellows. For those who consider that we need to begin picturing animals in a very different way (a position which is strong within relational approaches) we will need many concepts which are capable of performing many different roles. This may leave little scope for the sovereignty of any single concept, irrespective of which concept we happen to favour.

CONCLUSION

Although the political turn has not established a new orthodoxy in animal ethics, and is, indeed, very far from doing so, it has shown that there are ways to move on from the legacy of Singer and Regan which are very different from the alternatives offered by variously articulated forms of abolitionism. Whether or not, in the long run, it can sustain this difference is less clear. There is always the possibility that stepwise refinement of a Garner-style theory of justice, or of O'Sullivan's egalitarianism among animals, may begin to draw closer to a more cautiously formulated abolitionist standpoint, or else to the classical theories which the latter has sought to displace. Kymlicka's approach, by contrast, looks simultaneously more utopian and less vulnerable to any slippage in the direction of the established and rival discourses. However, it may purchase this distinctiveness at the cost of its utopian commitment. Yet it is intriguing to think that a stepwise refinement of key claims associated with the key political-turn texts might instead yield something capable of becoming a new, and more pragmatic, orthodoxy, or capable of presenting some account of an achievable animal liberation.

FURTHER READING

For the avoidance of cruelty as a key liberal norm, see Judith Shklar, *Ordinary Vices* (Cambridge, MA: Harvard University Press, 1984) and Richard Rorty, 'The Last Intellectual in Europe: Orwell on Cruelty', in *Contingency, Solidarity and Irony* (Cambridge: Cambridge University Press, 1989), 169–88. For a critique of this association between liberalism and cruelty avoidance, see John Kekes, 'Cruelty and Liberalism', *Ethics* 106(4) (1996): 834–44.

For the appeal to democracy and transparency as a basis for ending animal harms, see Siobhan O'Sullivan, *Animals, Equality and Democracy* (Basingstoke: Palgrave Macmillan, 2011). For the idea that some animals might be regarded as citizens see Sue Donaldson and Will Kymlicka, *Zoopolis: A Political Theory of Animal Rights* (Oxford: Oxford University Press, 2011). Their identification of problems in traditional rights theory builds on Claire Palmer's relational approach in *Animal Ethics in Context* (New York: Columbia University Press, 2010). For the more modest claim, that animals might be regarded as property-owners, see John Hadley, 'Nonhuman Animal Property: Reconciling Environmentalism and Animal Rights', *Journal of Social Philosophy* 36(3) (2005): 305–15. For an activist argument that the animal rights movement is best understood as a political movement rather than a moral crusade, see Kim Stallwood, *Growl: Life Lessons, Hard Truths and Bold Strategies from an Animal Advocate* (New York: Lantern Books, 2014).

For the inclusion of animals within a broadly liberal account of justice, see Robert Garner, *A Theory of Justice for Animals* (Oxford: Oxford University Press, 2013). Garner argues that the interest of animals in liberty is weak. For an extension of this into the claim that they have no direct interest in liberty, see Alasdair Cochrane, *Animal Rights without Liberation* (New York: Columbia University Press, 2012).

CONCLUSION

Animal ethics is currently in a state of transition. There is a widespread consensus that the first-wave theories of Singer and Regan, although insightful in many respects, have too many problems to form the basis for a viable and contemporary approach. They are the products of their time, and that time is not now. When it comes to ethics of any sort, Kantian and utilitarian approaches no longer seem like 'the only game in town', other options and influences need to be factored in. A heavy reliance on the argument from marginal cases, however formulated (in the manner of Singer or of Regan), also no longer seems like a wise move. Added to this, it is doubtful that any viable and contemporary animal ethic, one capable of responding to insights from multiple traditions, could afford to be quite so individualist and non-relational as the first-wave theories.

At the same time, it is not obvious what shape a successor approach will take, or whether animal ethics, or at least the kind of animal ethics which appeals to **animal advocates**, will ever again be so dominated by one or two closely allied positions. Perhaps **abolitionism**, if it continues on its current trajectory and fragments into competing formulations, will eventually generate a sufficiently conciliatory option, one which will be able to reach out more effectively beyond the ranks of existing animal advocates and beyond the US, in order to become the new orthodoxy that it has always aspired to be. But perhaps the more pragmatically inclined approaches associated with the **political turn** will slowly generate a new consensus which pushes the abolitionist approach steadily into the margins.

Alternatively, perhaps the latter will turn out to be just a little too pragmatic, a little too ready to integrate into existing political structures at a time when these structures are increasingly brought into question. Perhaps Donaldson and Kymlicka's less pragmatic articulation of the political turn should serve all such approaches as a cautionary note. Perhaps only a radically different political order of things could begin to accommodate a full measure of animal liberation or an extensive system of animal rights. More pragmatic approaches might then be torn between their readiness to work with the non-ideal and their commitment to remain motivated and guided by ideal aspirations. Keeping both in play without allowing one or the other to take over may prove to be difficult.

This does make our current time interesting for anyone working in animal ethics. But the possibility of a continuing shift into multiple, rival approaches, and the alternative possibility of the emergence of a new and more unified consensus, need not blind us to the considerable abiding strengths of the first-wave theories. It is not as yet clear just how different animal ethics is going to be in ten years time. Any plausible animal ethic, whether it sits alone or in the midst of rivals, may have to resemble the Singer and Regan approaches in significant respects. It may have to find a way to situate a conception of rights; it may have to acknowledge the centrality of interests; its conception of interests may have to connect up with an account of desires or preferences; its conception of interests may then have to acknowledge that humans often (not always) have interests which most animals do not; and, if it endorses some form of **species egalitarianism** as an alternative to **speciesism**, it may have to endorse a weak rather than strong version of such egalitarianism unless some way of rendering the strong version both plausible and liveable can be found. By general assent, a heavy reliance on the argument from marginal cases, together with an unqualified individualism, does now seem to be gone forever. Yet there may nonetheless be a productive return to other aspects of Singer and Regan.

GLOSSARY

Abolitionism The view that animal rights advocates ought only to campaign for the complete liberation of animals rather than for welfare reforms. On some variants, campaigning for the latter is permissible if the reforms themselves are deemed to be abolitionist, i.e. if they would end a practice rather than merely reforming it.

Analytic philosophy A tradition of philosophy primarily originating in English- and German-speaking countries which places emphasis on the logical analysis of arguments. In this respect it is taken to contrast with continental philosophy. (See below.)

Animal advocates Supporters of animal rights and/or animal liberation.

Animal liberation A term popularized by Peter Singer in his 1975 book of the same name, and signifying the ending of the most extensive forms of animal harms, especially those occurring in the food and experimental systems.

Anthropocentrism The view that humans have greater inherent value than non-humans, or treating humans *as if* they had greater inherent value than non-humans.

Argument from marginal cases (categorical version) The argument that *because* we would not harm humans in some way, given that they have some set of properties, we should also not harm animals in the same way if they have equivalent properties.

Argument from marginal cases (hypothetical version)   The argument that *if* we would not harm humans in some way, given that they have some set of properties, *then* we should not harm animals in the same way if they have equivalent properties.

Common good   The common good is the overall interest of a political community when the latter is thought of *as a community* and not simply as an aggregate of individuals.

Continental philosophy   A tradition in philosophy, influenced especially by French and German texts, which treats philosophy as (or as akin to) a form of literature and which is concerned especially with the articulation of positions rather than with formal argumentation. Contrasts with analytic philosophy. (See above.)

Doctrine of double-effect   The view that direct harms which are impermissible if intentionally caused, can nonetheless be justified, just so long as they are the unintended outcome of some action which aims at an important good.

Extinctionism   The view that domesticated creatures should be prevented from breeding in order to avoid future rights violations.

Greater value thesis   The claim that humans are of greater inherent value (see below) than non-humans.

Harm principle (Regan's version)   The view that we have a duty not to harm individuals who have inherent value. Not to be confused with John Stuart Mill's harm principle which governs when we are and are not allowed to impede the freedom of others.

Holism   The view that interrelated phenomena are, collectively, the basic unit of value or ethical significance. (Contrasts with individualism.)

Holocaust analogy   The claim that there is *something* strongly analogous between the Holocaust and our contemporary treatment of animals.

Individualism   The view that the bearers of value or ethical significance are individual beings or things. (Contrasts with holism.)

Inherent value   The value that something has in its own right.

Intrinsic value   The value that something has to a sentient being without consideration of any further advantage—e.g. an aesthetic experience could be intrinsically valuable to an agent.

Kantianism An approach to philosophical issues which draws from the tradition of Immanuel Kant (1724–1804). In ethical contexts this equates with an approach based on rights, duty and respect.

Land Ethic holism A form of holism (see above) which claims that what is right and wrong is determined by the impact that actions will have on the interests of ecosystems as a whole.

Maximin principle The principle that we should seek to maximize the position of the least well-off.

Miniride principle The principle that when we must fail someone, we should minimize the extent to which we do so, usually by failing in our duties towards the few rather than the many.

Moral agents Beings with a capacity to guide their actions through the exercise of autonomous choice in moral contexts.

Moral considerability Entitlement to non-instrumental consideration by moral agents. (See above.)

Moral extensionism The identification of some or other reason why humans matter followed by an argument that this will apply for similar reasons in the case of at least some non-humans.

Moral patients Beings who are incapable of guiding their actions through the exercise of autonomous choice in moral contexts.

Natural rights Rights which a human or animal has by virtue of its natural characteristics alone.

Naturalistic fallacy The most familiar understanding of the fallacy is that it involves the deriving of value claims ('ought' claims) exclusively from facts ('is' claims). However, rival interpretations have been offered. A familiar alternative is the view that this fallacy involves the construction of definitions in a way which makes two properties seem like one and the same property. And so a natural property and a quite different ethical property may then become confused.

Negative rights Entitlements to be left alone.

New welfarism ('welfarism' for short). A term used by abolitionists (see above) for any position which presents itself as supportive of animal rights or liberation while supporting reforms which modify but fail to abolish exploitative practices.

Open rescue A form of animal rights activism, pioneered in Australia and involving the apparently illegal, but open rather than covert, removal of animals from situations of harm.

Opportunity of life argument   The argument that without animal farming many animals simply would not be brought into existence and that animal slaughter and consumption is a fair price which animals pay in return for such an opportunity to live.

Original position   A situation in which agents deliberate about the rights and duties which will be acknowledged in a social contract. (For the latter, see below.)

Our common humanity   An ethically significant bond which is sometimes taken to exist between all humans and which plays a major role in the writings of Raimond Gaita and Gandhi. It is not to be confused with shared species membership but instead relates to patterns of entitlement and obligation.

Political turn   The political turn in animal ethics is a recent shift towards a more explicitly political understanding of how our relation to animals might be structured. It appeals to concepts associated with liberalism and democracy.

Positive rights   Entitlements to be enabled, assisted or compensated for some state of affairs.

Reflective equilibrium   An approach towards theory-building in ethics under which intuitions are used to constrain theories and theories are used to evaluate and sometimes correct the beliefs which we form on the basis of our intuitions.

Respect principle   Tom Regan's principle that creatures with inherent value are to be treated in ways which respect their inherent value.

Sentientism   The view that only sentient beings are morally considerable.

Slavery analogy   The analogy which is drawn (especially by abolitionists) between the current predicament of animals and the predicament of slaves in America's antebellum South.

Social contract   The idea that ethico-political rights and responsibilities have been fixed by a fair agreement or are best fixed by deliberation about what agents would agree to if they were to enter into such an agreement.

Sole value thesis   The claim that only humans have inherent value. (For the latter, see above.)

Species egalitarianism   The view that, at some level, all animals are equal.

Speciesism Favouring one species (usually humans) over another (usually non-humans). Some accounts require that this favouring must be directly justified or motivated by perceived species membership. Other accounts of speciesism suspend this requirement.

Strong species egalitarianism The view that animals and humans are equally important *and* that there is no additional reason to generally favour humans when human and animal interests clash.

Subjects-of-a-life Creatures which are not merely sentient but are moral agents (see above) have preferences and some level of self-awareness as well as an appreciation of their own existence over the course of time. This is a central concept in the writings of Tom Regan.

Supervenience A relation between high- and low-level properties such that a change in the former cannot occur without an associated change in the latter.

Utilitarianism An approach towards ethics which draws on the work of Jeremy Bentham (1748–1832) and John Stuart Mill (1806–1873). It aims at the maximizing of outcomes, in the sense of maximizing happiness, pleasure or the satisfaction of preferences.

Veil of ignorance A device used in thought experiments. Agents deliberating behind a veil of ignorance will lack knowledge of various things about themselves. What they lack ignorance of will be specified as part of the thought experiment.

Vivisection The performance of surgical procedures on animals for experimental purposes rather than for the animal's own good.

Weak species egalitarianism The view that animals and humans are equal in some respect or respects but that, in practice, humans will still tend to be prioritized over non-humans. This usually takes the form of arguing for the equal considerability of human and non-human interests but then accepting that humans typically have more of an interest in avoiding harms such as death.

Worse-off principle The principle that if we cannot avoid harming someone then we should harm the many rather than the few (or the one) whenever the latter happen(s) to be facing a greater prospect of harm.

INDEX